REMEMBERIN
AND THE

MW01690519

"We lived at 220 East Walton when Mrs. Thorne lived at 232 East Walton, so I often met her when she was walking to the Woman's Exchange on Michigan Avenue. She made and sold many rooms for the shop's benefit. They were much sought after. Many ladies of the neighborhood purchased them and they became cherished possessions.

"Mrs. Thorne was a charming, witty and excellent speaker. She used to give lectures at the Little Traveler Shop in Geneva, Illinois. I heard her speak on how to use paper and other materials to wrap Christmas packages.

"Her son, Niblack (always called Bill), was a friend of my husband's. They shared a mutual interest in rare books and antique cars."
—Peggy Carr, Grande Dame of Chicago

"I will never forget the first time my grandmother took me downtown from Oak Park on the Lake Street 'L' to the Art Institute to see the Thorne Rooms. I imagined myself living in each room as I stared into the small windows.

"Over the years I have taken my children and grandchildren to see them. All of us are continually 'awed' by the tiny replicas of rooms from many time periods."***—Caroline Freivogel, Miniaturist***

"When I was taken to see 'the rooms' as a girl, I imagined each of them as a brilliant stage set—elegant people standing in the wings, some intrigue about to unfold. My favorite scene was the modern French library, which opened onto a balcony that overlooked Paris. Breakfast—for two?—had already been set. High drama!

"I later learned that my young impressions had not been far off the mark. I grew up in Park Ridge, Illinois where Eugene Kupjack, the craftsman who had an omnipresent hand in Mrs. Thorne's American Rooms, also lived. It's interesting to read an early news story about his brother, Raymond, who was a painter. He said that the boys had attended grade school on Chicago's north side, where a teacher with a deep interest in drama took them to the opera. She wrote simpler versions of the music which the students could perform. The artistically talented Kupjack brothers worked out appropriate stage scenery and effects. Later, Eugene Kupjack told a reporter that his first ambition had been to design sets for the movies. This confirmed my impression that he and Mrs. Thorne and all of her artisans brought a grand theatrical sense to the creation of these famous miniature rooms.

"The Park Ridge Public Library has on permanent display one of the many miniature scenes Eugene Kupjack made for other collectors and institutions. It's fitting that Kupjack has now achieved a lasting celebrity of his own."***—Celia Hilliard, Chicago Author and Historian***

"My fondness for Thorne Rooms developed, like many people's, as a young child on visits to the Art Institute of Chicago with my mother. We would take frequent trips and always made a special pilgrimage to see the rooms. This may be a part of the reason why I now sell furniture! We sometimes have the privilege of handling a Thorne Room or other miniatures made by Mrs. Thorne, and it is always a treat to come across them. Her work is timeless, very Chicago. People value them for their historical accuracy as much as their exquisite craftsmanship."
—Leslie Hindman, Chicago Auctioneer

"I grew up in San Diego and my mother, Katherine, and my Aunt Narcissa—namesake of *her* aunt, Narcissa Thorne—would get together and reminisce about their childhood in Lake Forest. I remember stories about Aunt Narcissa contracting with hundreds of artisans and craftsmen all over Europe to make furniture and objects d'art for the miniature rooms.

"She wanted family members to participate in her projects, if even in a small way. Therefore, my mother and her sister were instructed to needlepoint and/or sew a little rug or wall-hanging to contribute to their aunt's cause—tasks that were more of a chore than a pleasure! They couldn't attend parties or ride their ponies until they showed progress on their assignments.

"They also saw some of the rooms being built and when they began to grow in number, the rooms were assigned to different family locations. Mom said she could actually see over time how her Aunt Narcissa developed a room that was to be kept at our house."***—Rudy Knepper, Great-nephew of Mrs. Thorne***

"My Grandfather realized I was interested in architecture and he would drive me around Hinsdale pointing out buildings in the Georgian style or Victorian or Prairie or Modern, etc. then would test me to see if I could spot the elements of what made a building one style or another. Once he felt I had somewhat mastered this he said, 'Now let's think about what these buildings look like inside,' and he took me off to the Art Institute to see the Thorne Rooms. There he showed me the various types of internal architecture and the furnishings that went with each style. He was impressed with Mrs. Thorne's skill in making these series of 'treasures,' as he called them, and they certainly are. He felt her work represented what education should be all about and that is the intellectual pursuit of knowledge while also learning to work with your hands to build things yourself.

"These trips were terrific learning opportunities and great fun. I never became a qualified architect but along with my wife, Kay, I've spent years remodeling one old house after another. I often think back on what Grandfather taught me so many years ago."—***Fred Krehbiel, Former CEO, Molex, Inc. and a collector of Thorne Rooms***

"In 1960, I returned to Chicago from several years of military service in the Far East and chose to live downtown instead of with the family in Winnetka. By then my siblings had returned to Chicago as well. My mother gave us a life membership in the Chicago Historical Society and the Art Institute of Chicago. I fondly remember the Society's dioramas and the Thorne Rooms at the Art Institute. Both were effective, but the Thorne Rooms, I thought, were more complete and instructive than the actual period rooms on display at that time."—***John Notz, Local History Buff***

"When I was a little girl, I had a cousin whose father built a dollhouse for her. I thought it was the greatest thing since sliced bread!

"I was always in awe of Mrs. Thorne. She and Mr. Kupjack made you believe you could walk into those rooms, sit down on the chairs, admire each piece of furniture and all the details of the period. That was my hook into miniatures. After hundreds of visits to the Thorne Rooms, I decided it would be great fun to collect miniatures and build a dollhouse for my granddaughter, Courtney.

"I became an avid hunter for about two years. I also started taking her to the Art Institute to visit the Thorne Rooms. When Courtney was six, Santa left a dollhouse that she could call her very own. (Yes, Virginia, there is a Santa Claus!)"—***Colette Pollock, Miniaturist***

“I remember well the first time I saw the Thorne Rooms. It was during a school field trip to the Art Institute in the late 1970s. In spite of everything I saw that day, the rooms made the greatest impression on me. I was already developing a strong interest in historic architecture, so they were an opportunity to step back in time, literally. I could imagine myself (a *much* smaller version of myself!) walking into the rooms and absorbing every last detail, from the ornamentation and furnishings to the way in which the ‘sunlight’ streamed through the windows.

“Nearly 20 years later, I learned about a dollhouse that my great-grandfather, also named William Tyre, had constructed for his daughter in 1898. Through some sleuthing I was able to locate and acquire the house, which by that time was in desperate need of restoration. I realized that it would never look as good as the Thorne Rooms, but I was inspired by Mrs. Thorne’s extraordinary attention to detail in selecting quality furnishings and architectural appointments to create my own little world of the 1890s.”—***William Tyre, Executive Director and Curator, Glessner House Museum***

“For a very fast 13 years, I was the ‘Technical Assistant’ for the Thorne Rooms at the Art Institute of Chicago. It was my responsibility to see to it that each room remained exactly as Mrs. Thorne had created it.

“I was their ‘cleaning lady in miniature,’ taking care of accumulated dust, polishing silver and brass, cleaning chandeliers—all just as you would do in your own home, except everything is so *tiny*! The scale of one inch to one foot required the greatest of care and skill.

“Everything stayed just where Mrs. Thorne had directed when she gave these delicate objects to our fabulous museum. Her original pictures tell us where everything is to be put, and this I followed to a tee. During my last year of employment, each piece of fabric and each textile was cleaned under the careful guidance of our Textile Department. Countless years of dust and dirt were removed.

“I have always been fascinated with miniatures, which I started collecting when I was of single digit age. I still add to my many, many collections. My mother-in-law was Colleen Moore Hargrave of the Fairy Castle fame, and her best friend was Narcissa Thorne. The extraordinary opportunity to care for the Thorne Rooms has been a great highlight of my life, one that I shall cherish always.”—***Alice Pirie Hargrave Wirtz, Technical Assistant, Thorne Rooms at the Art Institute of Chicago***

MRS. THORNE'S WORLD OF MINIATURES

SALLY SEXTON KALMBACH

AMP&RSAND, INC.
Chicago • New Orleans

ISBN 978-0-9905603-3-3

First Edition September 2014

DESIGN
David Robson, Robson Design

PUBLISHED BY
Ampersand, Inc.
1050 North State Street
Chicago, Illinois 60610

---

203 Finland Place
New Orleans, Louisiana 70131

www.ampersandworks.com

Printed in U.S.A.

The typefaces used in this book are New Caledonia,
a modern version of the popular 1890s typeface Scotch Roman,
and Sackers Gothic, based on old engraving type styles.

ON THE COVER
Mrs. James Ward Thorne (1882–1966)
(Courtesy of Anne Thorne Weaver)

ACKNOWLEDGEMENTS

In 1930, when Mrs. Thorne was enthusiastically constructing the first 12 miniature rooms, she said it was "with sublime ignorance of what a tremendous task I was preparing for myself." As I explored numerous paths seeking to provide an accurate account of Mrs. Thorne's life, I could identify with her statement.

Fortunately, I had the enormous aid of Mrs. Thorne's beloved granddaughter, Anne Thorne Weaver, to whom this book is dedicated. She provided me with private papers, pictures, speeches, letters, and notes that told Mrs. Thorne's own story. Many friends, too numerous to mention, encouraged me to write the story of Mrs. James Ward Thorne. Several provided immeasurable help: Susan Beré, Kevin Craig, Jean Fetridge, Caroline Freivogel, Robert Herbst, Suzanne Isaacs, Rudy and Sue Knepper, Lindsay Mican Morgan, David Robson, Deborah and William Sexton and Anne Thorne Weaver.

A special thank you to my husband, John; Elizabeth Kalmbach; Will and Kelly Kalmbach; and Amy Louise and James Peckham.

And I must not forget my granddaughter, Lucy Peckham, who loved throwing papers around my office.

Thank you for making this book possible.

Sally Sexton Kalmbach
Chicago, 2014

FOREWORD

In the early- to mid-20th century, Mrs. James Ward Thorne created the residential Thorne Rooms, accurate to the period of each room in every detail. They are found today at the Art Institute of Chicago, The Phoenix Art Museum, the Knoxville Museum of Art, the Indianapolis Museum of Art and the Museum of Miniature Houses (Carmel, Indiana). These rooms reflect trends of previous eras.

In the second decade of the 20th century, when Mrs. Thorne was completing her summer place in Lake Forest, Illinois with architects Edwin Hill Clark and William Otis, she continued the fashion by having rooms in her house decorated in styles of various periods from various nations. In his 1915 book, *Interior Decoration: Its Principles and Practice* (Doubleday), Frank Alvah Parsons outlined the characteristics of these national styles and their connotations. Parsons found French classicism a reflection of centralized order as seen at Versailles, which was ruled by the Sun King. By contrast, the English Tudor style, a reprise of medieval elements—linen-fold paneling, perpendicular arches—was designed for upwardly mobile classes from the late 1400s to the beginning of the 1600s, reflecting a decentralized and shifting distribution of power and wealth. A similar trend would follow with the entrepreneurial Dutch styles that came to England with the reign of William and Mary in the late 1600s. These domestic Gothic and more classic English styles came to America, the former to early New England and later the latter to New England as well as Virginia.

For Narcissa Niblack Thorne, these styles spoke of domestic patterns of living—kitchens, dining rooms, withdrawing rooms and bedrooms with various levels of formality—along with contrasting casual cottage or colonial and frontier settings. The carefully wrought details of walls, windows, floors and exteriors, glimpsed through window and door openings, gave a shimmering bright life to the spirits of these various historic and national systems of decoration.

By the 1920s, American homes were not made up of rooms in varying styles, but followed the Beaux Arts trend. The harmony of exterior, interior and gardens, as put forward in the 1897 book, *The Decoration of Houses* by Edith Wharton and Ogden Codman (Scribner's), was a more scholarly unity that characterizes Mrs. Thorne's approach, especially observable in the garden settings, which she carried out with precise detail and consistency.

In Chicago, specimens of decoration—such as Regency shop windows and paneled rooms—were donated and acquired in the 1920s era of architects Howard Van Doren Shaw and David Adler. Alas, exemplary works of these great Chicago architects did not survive the modernist house-cleaning of the 1950s. But the Thorne Rooms live on, preserved and lovingly restored, as windows into a time and place where past waves of culture and power can, to this day, inform and fascinate Chicago's citizens as well as those in Phoenix, Knoxville, Indianapolis and Carmel, Indiana.

This book tells the story of Narcissa Niblick Thorne in great detail and is a valuable contribution to the history of the Thorne Rooms, wherever they may be.

Arthur H. Miller, Chicago Historian and
Former Archivist, Lake Forest (Illinois) College

Mrs. Thorne holding her beloved granddaughter, Anne Thorne Weaver, on the terrace of her Santa Barbara home. (Courtesy of Anne Thorne Weaver)

CONTENTS

Collecting Miniatures 15
Setting the Stage 25
Travels to Europe and Inspiration for the First Miniature Rooms 37
First Set of Rooms Makes Its Debut 47
A Hobby Becomes a Mania 61
The American Story 81
Philanthropy 91
The Story Continues 105
Time Line 114
Bibliography 116
About the Author 120

LIST OF ILLUSTRATIONS

Mrs. James Ward Thorne ..... Cover
Mrs. Thorne and her granddaughter 10
Narcissa Thorne, circa 1907 14
White House in Miniature 17
Hall of the Guilds in Titania's Palace 18
Queen Mary with Sir Nevile Wilkinson, his wife and daughter 19
Queen Mary's Dolls' House in Sir Edwin Lutyens' drawing room 20
Chippendale Library designed by Kitty Carlisle 21
Colleen Moore 23
Narcissa's wedding picture, 1901 24
Frances Niblack with children 26
Narcissa Niblack, circa 1890 27
Mrs. Thorne with sons, circa 1912 30
The Thorne house and twin townhouses for the Glessner children 31
Lake Forest country house 32
Thorne apartment, 1200 North Lake Shore Drive 34
Thorne family, early 1920s 36
Bill Thorne in front of Lake Forest House 36
James Ward Thorne 39
Venetian Salon 40
Spanish Vaulted Hall 41
Santa Barbara home, "Montjoie" 42
Table setting at the Thorne Santa Barbara home 43
Louis XVI Dining Room 44
English Victorian Parlor 45
American Summer Kitchen–1885 48
Letter from W. Russell Button of Ackermann Galleries, 1932 50
Letter from New York architect William Adams Delano, 1932 52
Invitation to attend miniature room exhibit, 1932 53
"Streets of Paris" at the Century of Progress World's Fair, 1933 55
French Breton Kitchen 56

Chapter One of a proposed book about Thorne Miniature Rooms 59
Mrs. Thorne in the garden of her Santa Barbara home 60
Knole House, Kent, England 63
Belton House, Lincolnshire, England 64
Belton House carving by Grinling Gibbons 65
Double Cube Room, Wilton House 66
West facade of Wilton House, Salisbury, England 67
Georgian Library 70
Letter from the Victoria and Albert Museum, 1935 73
Queen Mary's thank you letter to Mrs. Thorne, 1937 75
Letter from Potter Palmer II, 1938 79
Mrs. Thorne in her studio 80
Mrs. Thorne in the Art Institute of Chicago 86
Letter from cartoonist John T. McCutcheon 89
Memorial to Mr. James Ward Thorne 90
Passavant Christmas Bazaar, 1960 92
Italian crèche, Passavant Hospital 95
Plaque honoring James Ward Thorne, 1949 96
Narcissa Thorne admiring a nurse's uniform, Passavant Hospital 98
Student Nurses' Library, Passavant Hospital 99
Awards and honorary degrees 101
Letter to IBM from Mr. James Ward Thorne, 1943 102
Letter written by Hans Huth, 1959 103
Mrs. Thorne, Arizona Biltmore Hotel, circa 1949–52 104
Shadow Box donated to the Woman's Athletic Club 106
Dining room 107
German Hallway 108
Miniature room designed by Sophia Twaddell 111
Narcissa Thorne, granddaughter and great granddaughter, 1953 113
English Reception Room of the Jacobean Period .... Back Cover

Narcissa Thorne around 1907. (Courtesy of Anne Thorne Weaver)

CHAPTER 1

COLLECTING MINIATURES

"Have a hobby for it's the greatest fun in the world, said Mrs. Thorne. My advice to every boy and girl is to start collecting something—stamps, books, dolls, anything which particularly appeals."

Mrs. James Ward Thorne
San Francisco News
September 1, 1938

People of all ages have long been fascinated with tiny, artistic items. Small versions of everyday objects have been produced for commercial and entertainment purposes throughout history. The earliest miniatures were found in Egyptian tombs dating from 3 B.C. The Egyptians buried their dead with items they might need or want in the afterlife. Depending upon one's wealth, the clay items varied from basic tools, pottery and food, to elaborate jewelry and furniture.

In the 17th century, craftsmen in Germany, Holland and England designed miniature houses to serve as examples of different styles of architecture and interior designs of the day. These houses displayed highly-crafted miniatures of actual furnishings. Wealthy clients could purchase the real thing and once their contracts were fulfilled, the miniature house became a catalogue of belongings, illustrating the owner's wealth.

Until the early 20th century, traveling salesmen carried miniatures of household furnishings like beds, chairs and dressers door-to-door in order to sell items to a broad group of middle class consumers. In many cases, to entice customers to buy, the small models were made of the same wood and displayed similar detailed workmanship as the larger versions.

Over time modern advertising and the increasing use of catalogues from Sears and Montgomery Ward greatly diminished the need for traveling salesmen and production of these miniatures diminished, too.

It was not until just prior to the 1930s and the Great Depression that miniatures gained recognition as significant collectibles. The Depression led families and stores to liquidate their holdings and antique miniatures became available at prices far more favorable than in previous years. At the same time, many unemployed skilled craftsmen and architects accepted commissions to create new examples of miniature goods. One of the highlights of the Chicago World's Fair of 1933–34 was the exhibit featuring the furnished period models of European and American Rooms designed by Mrs. James Ward Thorne of Chicago. Visitors waited in long lines to view the tiny rooms, all built on a scale of one inch to one foot. They caused quite a stir, and Mrs. Thorne's rooms became internationally known.

Many collectors from all over the world began building models of dollhouses, castles and period rooms to hold their vast numbers of miniatures. Their dedication provided a legacy for us to enjoy for years to come.

JOHN AND JAN ZWEIFEL

The largest dollhouse is one that all Americans can appreciate. It is a replica of a house owned by the American people: The White House in Washington, D.C.

An amazing story began in 1956 when a young man named John Zweifel took a public tour of the White House and decided he wanted to build a miniature copy. Zweifel was a confirmed model maker and miniaturist and felt that a miniature traveling version would provide an opportunity for thousands to view the White House.

He and his wife, Jan, an interior decorator, contacted the Kennedy White House in 1962 to discuss their idea. The staff was enthusiastic and the couple was given free access to photograph and sketch the rooms—a privilege that would never be granted today.

The Zweifels were on their way to accomplishing a herculean task, but needed additional visits. Unfortunately, tragedy struck. President Kennedy's assassination curtailed their access to the White House. It wasn't until 1975, during the Ford administration, that they were invited to continue gathering all the information they needed to build the 60 feet wide by 20 feet deep 10 ton "miniature" house that has traveled the nation since its completion in 1980.

Over 44 million people have enjoyed viewing the East and West Wings, Lincoln bedroom, Jackie Kennedy's garden, as well as the up-to-date Oval Office, which is redecorated whenever a new president takes

White House in Miniature. (*Courtesy of John and Jan Zweifel*)

office. The house has traveled to every state in the Union and many European countries, but today its permanent home is in the President's Hall in Claremont, Florida.

SIR NEVILE WILKINSON

One of the most fascinating dollhouses ever built is the result of a collaboration between a father and his young daughter. In 1907, just outside Dublin, Sir Nevile Wilkinson, a retired soldier, was working on a new career as an artist and children's author. When his three-year-old daughter, Gwendolen, told her father that she had spotted a fairy in the garden, his response made perfect sense. "Let us build a magnificent palace and see if we can lure the fairies out to stay!"

Fifteen years later their Italian Renaissance Palace was considered complete and was opened to the public in 1922. It contained 16 rooms with a belfry designed by Sir Edwin Lutyens, who also designed Queen Mary's dollhouse. They decided upon the name "Titania's Palace"—appropriate because Titania is the wife of Oberon, King of the Fairies!

Hall of the Guilds in Titania's Palace. (Courtesy of The New York Public Library)

The rooms were filled with antiques, hand-crafted furniture, paintings by Sir Nevile Wilkinson and gifts from Queen Mary, whose dollhouse had opened during the same time period in England. Queen Mary donated the china for the Royal Bedchamber so that Titania could enjoy a cup of tea first thing in the morning.

The Wilkinson Family had devoted many years to the palace's creation and wanted to share the result with children of all ages. The family sent the palace on a global tour for four decades, raising money for children's charities. Today Titania's Palace is housed in Egeskov Castle in Denmark.

Queen Mary with Sir Nevile Wilkinson, his wife Lady Beatrix, and daughter Gwendolen. (Courtesy of Library of Congress)

QUEEN MARY

At the same time that the Wilkinsons were completing their fairy castle, Princess Marie Louise, Queen Victoria's granddaughter, was organizing a fantastic gift for her childhood friend, Queen Mary. The princess was

Queen Mary's Dolls' House in Sir Edwin Lutyens' drawing room. (*Courtesy of Country Life Picture Library*)

well aware of her friend's love of tiny treasures and wanted to present Queen Mary and King George V with a gift in honor of their courage and leadership during World War I. Princess Marie Louise contacted the famous architect Edwin Lutyens to "devise and design for all time something which will enable future generations to see how a King and

Chippendale Library designed by Kitty Carlisle.(Courtesy of the National Trust UK)

Queen of England lived in the 20th century, and showcase the authors, artists, and craftsmen of note who existed during their reign."

Lutyens was not excited about the project initially, but became intrigued with the idea of a gift that would restore national pride and be exhibited at the 1924 British Empire Exhibition at Wembley Park, London.

The shell of the dollhouse was moved to Lutyens's residence in Mansfield Park, London and was constructed in his drawing room, depriving the family's use of the room for over two years! The project provided the opportunity for Lutyens to work with his 13-year-old daughter, Mary. She became an important helper, unpacking tiny objects to be housed in the dollhouse. This dollhouse represented another collaboration between a father and daughter.

When it was completed in 1924, Queen Mary said it was "The most perfect present anyone could receive."

Since 1925 the dollhouse has been located in Windsor Castle. It is visited by people from all nations and is considered to be the most wonderful dollhouse in the world.

KITTY CARLISLE

Kitty Carlisle started collecting miniatures in the 1890s as a young girl living in Calcutta. After her marriage she settled in South Kensington, London and frequented antique shops on Beauchamp Place, collecting bargains and bragging that she never paid more than half a crown (approximately 50¢) for any item. But she did pay for the items, unlike Queen Mary, who would often acquire miniatures by admiring other people's treasures. If she mentioned that she liked something, her loyal subjects felt obligated to present it to the queen as a gift. Soon word spread and households anticipating a visit from Queen Mary would hide all their "tiny craft!"

Carlisle visited the Queen's dollhouse around the same time period as Mrs. James Ward Thorne, and was so inspired that she decided to create period rooms for her collection of antiques. Many of her pieces were 18th century traveling salesmen's samples of chairs, chests, and beds.

After seeing Frank Early's woodwork in Queen Mary's dollhouse, Carlisle contacted him to create her Queen Anne Drawing room. It contains a walnut writing bureau with secret drawers and ivory handles with keys that turn in their locks.

The mahogany paneled Chippendale library created by Early is magnificent with its bookcase, library steps, stack of *The Times* newspaper and *Tatler* magazine, and an 18th century globe in its original brass case.

She continued to create the rooms over several decades on a scale of one-eighth to one foot, larger than the customary one inch (one-twelfth) to one foot made popular by Mrs. James Ward Thorne.

"It's unique," Mrs. Carlisle often said of her collection. Today the Carlisle Collection can be visited at the National Trust property, Nunnington Hall, outside of North Yorkshire, England.

COLLEEN MOORE

Kathleen Morrison was born in Michigan and grew up with two loves: dollhouses and the theater. Her father, Charles Morrison, commissioned several dollhouses for his only daughter and later launched her film career.

She entered the world of silent films in Hollywood as a teenager (at the same time as Mary Pickford) with the stage name of Colleen Moore. Her lucrative career spanned 20 years. Unfortunately, she was not as lucky in love and her first marriage collapsed in 1930.

Realizing that his beloved daughter was depressed in an unhappy marriage, Charles Morrison suggested that they "design and build a fairy castle to end all fairy castles!" They hired the finest craftsmen from Hollywood and Charles Morrison used his own skills as an engineer to oversee the project.

This collaboration between father and daughter took seven years, cost more than $500,000, and contains more than 2,000 miniature objects. Completed in 1935, it depicts well-known fairy tale themes and boasts its own magic garden. Friends and family eagerly contributed to making the castle an artistic achievement.

Colleen Moore (Courtesy of Library of Congress)

European and Egyptian antiquities, a chandelier made out of Moore's own diamond and emerald jewelry, hollow glass slippers for Cinderella, a pistol that fires tiny silver bullets, and chair back clips made of jewels that once decorated one of Moore's jackets are just a few of the sumptuous items that decorate the fairy castle.

Clare Booth Luce, playwright and Congresswoman, donated a medallion containing a piece from the cross of Jesus that she received from the Pope. Luce offered it as a tribute to her young daughter who had been killed in a car accident.

After the dream castle was completed in 1935, it began a national tour to benefit children's charities. During this time Moore met Chicagoan Homer Hargrave, married him and became actively involved at the Art Institute of Chicago and Museum of Science and Industry. In 1949 the Fairy Castle was displayed at the Museum of Science and Industry and in 1976 it became a permanent exhibit.

Colleen Moore's move to Chicago and her work with the city's museums brought her face-to-face with a fellow miniature enthusiast named Mrs. James Ward Thorne. Their friendship was based on a common love of miniatures and both women left a lasting legacy through their unique work in the field.

Narcissa's wedding picture, 1901. (Courtesy of Anne Thorne Weaver)

CHAPTER 2

SETTING THE STAGE

"She keeps a large house on a small scale."
St. Louis Dispatch
April 26, 1944

Narcissa Niblack started collecting miniatures when she was a young girl. As an adult, Mrs. James Ward Thorne's hobby turned into a full-time project. For 15 years she designed and created dollhouses for all of the little girls in the family and wards of several children's hospitals. They were large and complete dollhouses. As her enthusiasm for interior design increased, the houses became more and more sophisticated.

Mrs. Thorne decided she might develop some interesting way of making rooms in miniature which could be exhibited in museums as an educational tool for students of architecture and interior design. The result was a gift for Chicago and the world when she donated a series of miniature period rooms to the Art Institute of Chicago. The European and American Rooms were permanently installed in their own gallery, providing an accurate history of architecture and interior design as well as a history of domestic life.

Narcissa Niblack was born in Vincennes, Indiana on May 2, 1882. She was the eldest of three children.

Her mother, Frances Caldwell, was descended from a milling family in Virginia, and her father, William, was descended from Mayflower passengers who settled in Salem, Massachusetts.

Her sister, Lydia, married Alden Swift of the Chicago meat-packing industry and her brother, Austin, married Helen Cudahy, a member of another Chicago meat-packing family.

Narcissa started collecting miniatures as a child and was encouraged by her uncle, Rear Admiral Albert Niblack. He brought Narcissa

Frances Niblack with children Narcissa, Austin, and Lydia.
(Courtesy of Anne Thorne Weaver)

souvenirs of tiny furniture, vases, silver, and tea sets from his U.S. Navy tours abroad.

Mrs. Thorne said, when interviewed:

> "When I was a small girl, I had a tall, jolly uncle who loved teenie-weenie things. He traveled all over the world and when he came back from his exciting adventures, he always brought me the most interesting presents. These lovely little gifts were the inspiration for my collection of miniature things. I kept everything tucked away in boxes. Then one Christmas, my mother gave me a mahogany cabinet, which looked as though it had been taken from the house of the seven dwarfs, for it was only three feet high and had four shelves and glass doors which locked with a small brass key. And I proudly transferred my collection there."

Narcissa Niblack around 1890. (Courtesy of Anne Thorne Weaver)

Narcissa became fascinated with dollhouses and, at the age of five, was given a four-room dollhouse designed by a local carpenter. Her artistic sense of detail must have already been intact because she said, "The general effect offended my sense of beauty and scale. The dolls sat in stiff discomfort on much too large chairs, and the fact that there was no stairway thoroughly disturbed me." But she was thrilled with a gift of a delicately made chair and table which held a silver tea set, all of accurate proportions and fine quality, which she received at about the same time. Thirty-five years later, Narcissa found an identical tea set in Paris and once again experienced pure enchantment.

Her dissatisfaction with her first dollhouse led Narcissa to make her own creations. Some were made from chocolate boxes, some from crates obtained from grocers, but all contained crudely built staircases. A serious desire to design and collect started in adolescence and her interest in interior design grew as she matured into a young woman.

In 1890 the family moved to Hyde Park in Chicago when her father assumed an important post at the Chicago Title and Trust Company. Chicago in 1890 had just won the bid to host the Columbian Exposition, but not without resistance from New York City. When the race was tied between the two cities, the *New York Sun* printed, "Pay no attention to the nonsensical claims of that windy city. Its people couldn't build a World's Fair if they won it." In spite of New York's accusations, Chicago's efforts proved successful and construction began in Jackson Park not far from the Niblack family's new home. It was an exciting time to live in the Hyde Park area, watching the Ferris wheel being built on the Midway, flanked by buildings of the newly opened University of Chicago, and the development of "The White City."

Narcissa continued her education at Kenwood Institute in Hyde Park. In later years she commented about her education. "The trouble with my childhood, I was given no education. Knowing how to put my hat on straight was supposed to be enough."

However, she traveled extensively with her parents in the United States and Europe, visiting numerous museums that would play a large part in her future hobby. In addition, Narcissa learned to speak Italian and French, which helped immensely when she was visiting small antique shops in France and Italy where no English was spoken.

Chicago in the mid-1890s was an active, developing metropolis of steel-framed skyscrapers. Cultural institutions such as the Art Institute and Auditorium Theater, and the developing business mecca called the Loop, were all features of one of the fastest growing cities in America.

At the age of 19, Narcissa married her childhood sweetheart, James Ward Thorne, son of George Thorne, co-founder of Montgomery Ward & Co. Founded in 1872, it was the first general merchandise mail-order catalogue company in the United States.

At the time of her marriage the feminine, blond, blue-eyed Narcissa was described as artistic, divinely tall and most divinely fair. The wedding on May 30th took place at Trinity Episcopal Church, and was described in "The Society World" of the *Chicago Daily Tribune*. Her wedding dress was made of white lace and satin with a long veil of white tulle fastened with a diamond star.

Narcissa's artistic streak was illustrated by her bridal bouquet—a number of small bunches of lilies of the valley tied together in white satin cascading down the front of her dress. The bridesmaids wore white dresses with pink sashes and carried big bunches of white peonies tied with pink streamers.

Shortly after their wedding reception, held at her family home in Hyde Park, the couple departed to spend the summer in Europe.

They returned to live in a house in Chicago's original silk stocking district, Prairie Avenue. Mrs. Thorne and her husband, an amateur woodworker and toy repairer, used a large, well-equipped room as a workshop. They both enjoyed working with their hands and decided to build dollhouses. One of their first ventures was to design a dollhouse for a favorite niece, one that contained a staircase rising through three stories! As a couple they became quite enthusiastic about their successes and continued to make additional houses of varied designs for friends, family, orphans' homes, and wards of childrens' hospitals. In time, the houses became more detailed in design and less appropriate for play.

Narcissa became an active fund-raiser for numerous organizations including the Art Institute of Chicago, Chicago Historical Society (now the Chicago History Museum), Children's Memorial Hospital (now the Ann & Robert H. Lurie Children's Hospital), and the Service Club, but she was especially involved with the Woman's Exchange. This group was established in Chicago in 1893 to give women part-time work outside of the home. The Exchange offered an opportunity for women to sell needlework, embroidery, and other objects to subsidize their income. Mrs. Thorne contributed numerous hand-made items to be sold at the Exchange for charitable purposes.

On one occasion a customer from the Exchange requested a dollhouse which Mrs. Thorne constructed of such superior quality and proficiency that it occupied a place of honor in the Exchange store's window on North Michigan Avenue. It attracted so much attention that orders for doll-houses sky-rocketed, and eventually, they became too numerous for her to fill so she sought outside help. When the Depression hit, Mrs. Thorne

Mrs. Thorne with Ward and Bill around 1912. (Courtesy of Anne Thorne Weaver)

ordered dollhouses from the prestigious New York architectural firm of Delano & Aldrich. The firm had begun making dollhouses to give workmen employment when the building business became extremely slow.

In later years, shadow boxes, dioramas, and knickknacks were all made by Mrs. Thorne in her studio at the Exchange shop. She provided financial support to the Exchange, and her leadership provided for the livelihood of numerous women. Many society women contributed by hosting

The Thorne house was to the south (left) of the twin townhouses for the Glessner children. The Thorne address was 1708 South Prairie. (Courtesy of William Tyre)

bazaars in their own homes, or at popular hotels, including the Drake and Blackstone, for the benefit of the Woman's Exchange.

Narcissa's volunteer work and steady collecting of miniatures took place as she was raising two sons—Ward born in 1902 and Niblack (called Bill) in 1905.

Mrs. Thorne was not the only woman working with miniatures on Prairie Avenue. Her neighbor and friend, Frances Glessner Lee, also constructed miniature representations. Frances was the daughter of John Glessner, partner in the firm Warder, Bushnell & Glessner, which merged with several firms in 1902 to become International Harvester.

The Glessners were a philanthropic family and became one of the founders of the Chicago Orchestra in 1891, led by Theodore Thomas, and re-named the Chicago Symphony Orchestra in 1913. They regularly attended the symphony, which was one of the joys in their lives.

Frances decided to design a hand-crafted miniature orchestra to present to her mother as a birthday gift on January 1, 1913. Initially the model was on display in the Glessner home and viewed by a large number of

Lake Forest country house designed by Edwin Clark and William Otis.

guests since the Glessners were avid entertainers. In 1921 the miniature model was donated to the Chicago Symphony Orchestra.

Mrs. John Glessner, Frances's mother, belonged to that rare group of strong women who left a lasting imprint on the city of Chicago. She co-founded the Chicago Chamber Music Society, and established the first local chapter of the Daughters of the American Revolution. She belonged to the Art Institute of Chicago and the Antiquarian Society.

In 1893 (the year of the Columbian Exposition) William Rainy Harper, president of the newly founded University of Chicago, approached Mrs. Glessner with a problem. He needed her help in introducing university faculty wives to women in the city of Chicago. Her solution was an innovative Monday Morning Reading Club to take place every other Monday from October until May. The Club hired a professional reader for the first hour during which the ladies generally sewed. The second hour was typically devoted to a lecture or music by Chicago Symphony members. While Mrs. Thorne was living on Prairie Avenue she joined the Club and it continued to meet at the Glessner home from 1893 until 1930.

Frances also worked on another miniature project vastly different from Narcissa's period rooms. Frances became interested in forensic pathology and created 18 dioramas of actual crime scenes entitled the "Nutshell Studies of Unexplained Death." They are still being used for training purposes by the Harvard Associates in Police Science.

While living on Prairie Avenue, the Thorne and Glessner families became good friends. The Thornes visited them at "The Rocks," their summer home in New Hampshire. It is fair to say that both ladies had much in common. Frances was only four years older than Narcissa, both raising young children during their time on Prairie Avenue. They lamented the fact that they had received little formal education. Creativity and an urge to work with their hands were paramount in their lives. Both had extensive rare book collections for research purposes that they later donated to libraries: Mrs. Thorne's to the Ryerson Library of the Art Institute and Frances Glessner Lee's to the library she had helped to establish—the George Burgess Magrath Library of Legal Medicine at Harvard University.

The work to which Narcissa and Frances dedicated themselves remains useful, and both "amateurs" became respected authorities in their fields. Today the Glessner House is a vibrant museum offering tours, lectures, and a wide variety of activities.

In 1910, Narcissa and James Thorne hired architects Edwin Clark and William Otis to design a country house for use on weekends and during the summer in Lake Forest. The town is located on the shores of Lake Michigan, 32 miles north of Chicago, and was founded around Lake Forest College in 1857. In the 1890s it had become a popular summer retreat for Chicagoans wanting to escape from the city.

Edwin Clark had designed many public buildings in the Chicago sub urbs, including the neo-Palladian Lake Forest Public Library, Winnetka Village Hall, Brookfield Zoo, Memorial Building in Hinsdale and several large estates on the North Shore of Lake Michigan.

The association with Clark proved successful and resulted in a French chateau-style home with formal gardens and an elaborate swimming pool in the Beaux-Arts style. Weekend guests enjoyed croquet, swimming, skeet shooting, and walking the extensive grounds of the estate.

The Thornes were so pleased with Clark's work that they contacted him in 1916 to design a library in their newly purchased apartment at 1200 North Lake Shore Drive in Chicago. The building was designed by Chicago architect Benjamin Marshall and was fashioned in the French style favored by Mrs. Thorne. Marshall's name had become synonymous with luxury apartment buildings and hotels. He designed the Drake and

Thorne apartment at 1200 North Lake Shore Drive designed by Benjamin Marshall. (Courtesy of Dr. Lynn Westley)

Blackstone hotels as well as the grand apartment buildings on East Lake Shore Drive. They remain today as a reminder of a by-gone era of large, well-designed apartments.

Marshall was a flamboyant figure who designed his own clothes and drove a white custom-made Packard. He socialized with important businessmen and members of society, but was especially fond of theater people. Marshall's lifelong enthusiasm for the theater is evident in his buildings. He infused a sense of the dramatic with spacious rooms and vistas in the apartments he designed. It is significant that Mrs. Thorne chose an apartment designed by Marshall to create what she called "tiny stage sets." It was in this apartment in 1930 that she built her first set of 12 rooms, which were introduced to the general public at the 1933–34 Century of Progress World's Fair.

While continuing to accumulate miniatures and design items for the Woman's Exchange, Mrs. Thorne started collecting rare books about interiors, architecture, and furniture. This was an untouched field in the early 1920s. Many of the early and rare books were written in an age before photography and only limited travel.

She dedicated herself to reading and researching all aspects of interior design—from Edith Wharton's book on interiors entitled *The Decoration of Houses* to first-edition, color-plated books supplemented by original drawings on period rooms and period furnishings. Chippendale, Hepplewhite, and Sheraton were styles that she studied while reading the 18th century *Gentleman's & Cabinet Maker's Directory* by Chippendale and *The Cabinet Maker's & Upholsterer's Drawing Book* by Thomas Sheraton.

Furniture, upholstery, landscape scenery, and landscape gardening were covered in Mrs. Thorne's collection of finely engraved book illustrations. According to a 1939 *San Francisco Examiner* story, Mrs. Thorne's library was considered one of the finest and best privately-owned libraries in the United States. In 1940 she presented her entire collection of color-plate books to the Department of Prints and Drawings at the Art Institute of Chicago. This group of illustrated volumes provided a history of the manners, art and costumes of the 19th century. The Ryerson Library of the Art Institute also received her collection of books about furniture, including volumes about 18th century English cabinetmakers as well as books about interiors and decorative arts which have been on display periodically over the years.

Top: Thorne family, early 1920s. Bottom: Bill Thorne in front of Lake Forest House. (Both photos courtesy of Anne Thorne Weaver)

CHAPTER 3

TRAVELS TO EUROPE AND INSPIRATION FOR THE FIRST MINIATURE ROOMS

"I was told in Europe one could find exquisite antique miniature furniture, made to very small scale, and with my mind groping for suggestions I went abroad to hunt in Italy and France for such pieces, to form a nucleus around which I could develop copies of old period rooms."

Mrs. Thorne's lecture during the Century of Progress World's Fair, 1933–34

The 1920s hit Chicago and the rest of the country with a bang. It was the beginning of an era of widespread prosperity following the somber mood of World War I. Dubbed "The Roaring '20s" and "The Jazz Age," it was a time when modern technology—the automobile, moving pictures, radio—began to take hold.

The long-awaited vote for women, a campaign that started in Seneca Falls, New York in 1848, became a reality with the passage of the 19th amendment.

It was also the beginning of an exciting new era for Chicago. The city called for a system of lakefront parks, beaches, yacht harbors, and improved road and rail transportation in and out of Chicago. Architect and city planner Daniel Burnham's Plan of 1909 was implemented in 1920 by building the Michigan Avenue Bridge and widening the street that eventually became known as the Magnificent Mile.

During this eventful time Mrs. Thorne continued her dedication to collecting books and miniatures.

Beginning in the early 1920s, she and her husband made several trips to Europe, but their travels increased when James Thorne retired from Montgomery Ward in 1926 at the age of 53. The couple spent months at a time traveling extensively throughout Europe, collecting miniatures from antique and curiosity shops.

> "My fondest recollection of Narcissa Thorne was in Europe where my family had an apartment in Paris in the late 1920s and 1930s. At that time she was busy refurbishing the dollhouse for Queen Mary in England. She stayed at the St. James Palace, and had interesting associations with the Royal family. She had a lot of charm and poise, and very interesting experiences."
>
> *Narcissa Thorne Kiewert*
> *Niece and namesake of Mrs. James Ward Thorne*

James Thorne, an amateur photographer, took pictures of the magnificent chateaux of Normandy and Brittany and the elegant English country homes open to the public. They visited the recently completed Queen Mary's dollhouse in Windsor, the Victoria & Albert Museum's collection of architectural models, and the Musée des Arts Décoratifs in Paris. It was in these venues that Mrs. Thorne first saw dollhouses that had become permanent displays.

"It seemed to me such a pity that there was no way of offering American students the opportunity of studying the exquisite architecture and interior detail of the English country house and French chateaux designs. In my mind's eye I certainly saw these great rooms in miniature scale—an *Alice in Wonderland* reduction."

Mrs. Thorne decided to develop interesting ways to make miniature rooms that could be exhibited in museums. The idea persisted while traveling in Europe. Up until this time only actual rooms were re-created in museums and restored in villages such as Williamsburg, Virginia. She realized she could take it a step beyond designing and building dollhouses and would not have to worry about the "lovely little ornaments and furniture being ruined by some destructive child!"

While visiting Rome in 1930, Mrs. Thorne was walking down a side street along the Tiber River when she spotted two exquisite tiny chandeliers made of bronze and semi-precious stones hanging in the window of an antique shop. The shop contained other treasures as well: gold mirrors, tables, and rare terra-cotta busts, all constructed on a scale of one inch to one foot.

She said of that visit: "I shall never forget my thrill of excitement as I entered that shop. They were real treasures, but when the prices were

James Ward Thorne. (Courtesy of Anne Thorne Weaver)

added into one enormous total, I drooped with bitter disappointment. No one could explain that extravagance to even the most understanding husband. It just wasn't sane. I returned to the hotel wishing that I had never started the quest of things in miniature."

After a night of little sleep and dreams of owning the lovely pieces, Mrs. Thorne returned to the shop the next day. She said: "Finally I could stand it no longer, the urge too great, some power, far stronger than my

Venetian Salon. The antique chandeliers were the inspiration for the first set of rooms. (Courtesy of Chicago History Museum)

will, pushed me to the door of the antique dealer's shop, and I bought the eight pieces. My joy over their possession knew no bounds, and that trip abroad will always be one of the most delightful memories of my life. It was the beginning of a new enthusiasm which has filled the last few years to overflow."

Soon Mrs. Thorne's eye became so trained to tiny objects that nothing escaped her notice. In a dusty shop window in Orvieto, Italy she discovered one inch high bottles in braided straw filled with red wine, exact replicas of the wine the Thornes had enjoyed for their picnic lunch. When she returned to their car, her husband asked, "Now what could you have found in that place?" She proudly produced the tiny wine bottles! They continued to travel through Tuscany adding to their collection, and Mrs. Thorne described those days as a "dream."

In Paris, the hunt continued in shops on the left bank of the Seine and the side streets of Montmartre where she discovered a Louis XVI desk with marble top, commodes, consoles, all of excellent workmanship with inlaid wood, antique hardware and working locks with tiny keys, all on the scale of one inch to one foot.

All of her purchases were displayed on the piano in the sitting room of their Paris hotel. The hotel maid was told not to touch any of the miniatures. Dusting was absolutely prohibited!

Spanish Vaulted Hall. The intricate ironwork was copied from original pieces in an old Spanish Hall. On permanent exhibit at the Knoxville Museum of Art. (Courtesy of Chicago History Museum)

When she left Paris, each miniature was painstakingly wrapped in tissue paper and packed in a trunk her husband had purchased especially for her collection. It took hours.

"When I landed at the American customs, I was prepared to spend the day on the dock. I had separated the antiques. The officer looked at these first, passed them at once, but when he started on the mass of tissue paper and cotton batting and undid six or eight articles, he said, 'Oh madam, I'll take your word for it.'"

She didn't realize how many miniatures she had purchased until she unpacked the trunk. Hundreds of items were added to an already large collection of miniatures at home, and ideas started to take shape as she formed them into groups. The chandeliers, bronze tables and mirrors purchased in Rome suggested a Venetian Salon. A carved credenza, Savonarola chairs and a refectory table laden with goblets, bowls and old plates of silver were reminiscent of a dining hall in the 14th century Palazzo Davanzati in Florence.

Water jars, wine bottles, and pottery miniatures collected during the trip reminded Mrs. Thorne of a picture she had seen of a Majorcan kitchen.

Two large bedrooms in the Thorne's Lake Shore Drive apartment that formerly were for her sons were turned into a workshop. She began the time-consuming project of constructing the first set of 12 period rooms.

Santa Barbara home named "Montjoie." (*Courtesy of Anne Thorne Weaver*)

Chests were filled with tiny trinkets and shelves along the wall held pots of paint, brushes, tweezers, etc. She worked tirelessly with great enthusiasm and also "with a sublime ignorance of what a tremendous task I was preparing for myself."

New ideas continued to form, sometimes inspired by one or two items discovered in a remote antique shop. A miniature ivory chess queen and a bust of a cardinal purchased on the isle of Capri became the impetus for a Spanish Vaulted Hall. Reproducing the intricate metal work chosen from models in architect Arthur Byne's book of photographs and drawings presented some problems.

Fortunately, in Santa Barbara, California, the location of the Thorne's new vacation home, she found numerous skilled artisans who could create the items in the Spanish Vaulted Hall and a Spanish Bedroom. Narcissa hired a Mexican man from the area who was able to reproduce architect Byne's delicate drawings of wrought iron grilles, fire screens, and candlesticks with perfect precision. At the same time she found an excellent Italian wood carver and arranged to take private classes from him to learn the techniques of woodworking. Together they designed and made pieces of furniture for the Italian and Spanish rooms.

Table setting at the Thorne Santa Barbara home featured in House and Garden *magazine. (Courtesy of Anne Thorne Weaver)*

In 1926, the year of James Ward Thorne's retirement, Narcissa and James had purchased a lot in Santa Barbara and once again hired architect Edwin Clark to design their Beaux Arts villa. The 10,000 square foot estate with views of the Pacific Ocean was completed in 1928 and named Montjoie, meaning "mountain of joy." Mrs. Thorne was intimately involved with the design of every room in the house, and her interest and knowledge of architecture was evident throughout. Rooms were modeled after 17th and 18th century European styles including an 18th century Parisian dining room, and a 17th century library paneled in walnut that came from a Tuscan Abbey. The 18th century Viennese ballroom contained marble fireplaces, beautifully intricate hardwood floors, and sweeping views of the ocean and mountains from the generous windows. When completed, several rooms of the house were featured in *House and Garden* magazine. In the same magazine issue Mrs. Thorne's creative expertise was illustrated in table settings on the terrace of her Santa Barbara home. One was set for a children's luncheon and had a long-eared donkey for a centerpiece, another for an informal tea, and the last displayed an elaborate silver tea set.

Louis XVI Dining Room. A reproduction of a room in a chateau in France. On permanent exhibit at the Phoenix Art Museum. (Courtesy of Chicago History Museum)

"She was especially fond of Louis XVI style and her dining room was rich and elaborate. I spent one summer at her home in Santa Barbara and she was wonderful to me."

Narcissa Thorne Kiewert
Niece and namesake of Mrs. James Ward Thorne

One day Mrs. Thorne was cleaning out the drawers of an old desk and found a roll of paper and some swatches of dusty wools. The paper contained a beautiful painting of an 18th century tapestry designed by Parisian Francois Boucher.

Mrs. Thorne's imagination allowed her to believe it was tucked into the hiding place by a lovely French Marquise to be found centuries later! Her miniature Louis XVI Dining Room took form from this discovery. Six exquisitely carved chairs and a table were made by a workman of the old school for this green and rose room. Mrs. Thorne said, "When he delivered them he gave me all manner of instruction regarding their care. I felt as if I were adopting several babies."

The Louis XVI Dining Room provided a home for amber glass, porcelains, and gold ornaments purchased from numerous Parisian shops. It also included an attempt at copying an Aubusson rug that kept Mrs. Thorne busy for many hours and nearly ruined her eyesight!

English Victorian Parlor. The furniture came from an old English dollhouse. On permanent exhibit at the Knoxville Museum of Art. (Courtesy of Chicago History Museum)

Enamored with the style of Louis XVI, Mrs. Thorne continued with the design of a French Boudoir. It contained two treasures; a little inlaid desk and commode from the Rue St. Honoré along with numerous ornaments found in shops along the Seine. The walls, door and mantel are copies of an authentic Empire style room of that period, and the furniture is reproduced from museum pieces. Upholstering the furniture and draping the taffeta curtains on the bias gave Mrs. Thorne "hours of nerve wracking work."

The furniture for the English Victorian Parlor came from an old English dollhouse. Additional pieces such as the Rockingham lamb came from the Close of the Canterbury Cathedral, the British coal scuttle from the Burlington Arcade in London, and a Leland print from Stratford-upon-Avon. But the massive chandelier presented difficulties. The globe for the gas had to be hand-blown, but the prisms for decoration were not to be found. Sometimes Mrs. Thorne was forced to make substitutions for common objects not available in miniature, and used her imagination to find the solution.

One spring morning she was walking past Woolworth's Five and Dime in Chicago and, on a whim, walked in. At the first counter she discovered hundreds of necklaces made of glass bugle beads, prefect for the chandelier. She purchased twenty strings, and the clerk looked at her as if she were crazy! When completed, the English Victorian Parlor was reminiscent of a room where you would have visited your grandmother or great aunt. Mrs. Thorne thought it would be the "clown of the collection," but it proved to be the general favorite.

SOUPÇON

In 1930, Montgomery Ward declined a merger offer from its rival, Sears Roebuck. The company had lost money during the Great Depression and hired Sewell Avery as President. He cut staff, closed stores, and revamped the company to make it more profitable. In 1939, a staff copywriter at Montgomery Ward created the character and illustrated the poem "Rudolph the Red-nosed Reindeer" as part of a promotional Christmas campaign.

The store distributed six million copies of the story. Seven years later, Gene Autry popularized the song.

After World War II, Montgomery Ward's sales declined, and Avery was blamed for not understanding the changing economy post-World War II.

CHAPTER 4

FIRST SET OF ROOMS MAKES ITS DEBUT

"Mrs. Thorne has done a great deal more than simply assemble the appropriate furnishings for the series of rooms. She has created that intangible quality, atmosphere, and feeling of place, which coupled with a supremely artistic color sense and regard for exactness of scale and proportion, make each one of the period rooms a work of art."

Edith Weigle
Chicago Sunday Tribune
June 8, 1941

The ideas were formulated for the first 12 rooms, furniture acquired and being made, but it was time for the designs of the rooms to be drawn. Because Mrs. Thorne had completed years of research in architecture and interior design, she was almost fanatical in wanting the rooms or "shells" to be architecturally correct in design, scale, and proportion. Architects Edwin Clark and Herbert Banse of Edwin Clark & Herbert Banse, Inc. drew the architectural designs for the rooms that were built by the Francis W. Kramer Studios in Chicago. Both architects designed some of the early buildings of Brookfield Zoo, Lake Forest public library, and several buildings for the Century of Progress World's Fair in 1933–34.

After the blueprints of the rooms were completed to her detailed specifications, Kramer Studios built boxes ranging from two to three feet long and from 18″ to 20″ deep. Mrs. Thorne worked with several skilled artisans on the interiors, adhering to a scale of one inch to one foot. Initially, she designed rooms based on her research of the finest type of room of each period.

She utilized her excellent library of reference books, drawings, and photographs to work with the craftsmen, marbleizing floors, upholstering

American Summer Kitchen–1885. On the left wall hangs a copy of the Montgomery Ward & Co. catalogue. On permanent exhibit at the Knoxville Museum of Art. (Courtesy of Chicago History Museum)

chairs, and painting rooms. A skilled needlewoman, she embroidered fine petit point. Mrs. Thorne designated where every piece of furniture was to be placed. In some rooms there were as many as 134 items.

As the 12 rooms were nearing completion, Mrs. Thorne felt something was missing. "I realized what was disturbing me. They had no life, no atmosphere. Then I saw what was wrong. I had put glass in the windows and the curtains were beautifully made and very convincing, but no light came through the windows, which was completely unnatural. My chauffeur (who worked for Mrs. Thorne for 45 years) helped me solve the problem by placing an electric bulb not far from the window opening on the outside. I turned on the center lights in my studio, and instantly there was the effect I wanted—sunshine coming through the window, putting life and a third dimension into my model.

"From then on I worked with the lighting effects in mind, planning gardens or street scenes visible through the windows. This gave me a chance to add authentic touches. I think creating the gardens was as much fun and required as much ingenuity as making the rooms themselves."

From the English Victorian Parlor one looks out at a street in Oxford. From the warm Salem Kitchen one views a New England snow scene. Through the Spanish Vaulted Hall a fountain with a formal garden is seen in the background. The light changes from early morning sunrise to an evening scene where from one room you can see the Palmolive Building in Chicago with its famous Lindbergh Beacon lit at night.

But her favorite was the view from the tall windows of the French Boudoir which offered a scene of Paris overlooking the flower-filled balconies of the city.

During the winter of 1932, while Mrs. Thorne was busy diligently completing the first 12 miniature rooms, she was also organizing a winter exhibit of her collection of color plate books and original drawings at the Art Institute of Chicago. The rare book and print collections, largely from the 18th and 19th centuries, included books on travel, scenery, English topography, architecture, caricature and costume, and color plate books by Rowlandson and Cruikshank, Leech, Nash and Phiz. One of the world's most elaborate and rare gold-lettered books, *The Coronation of George IV*, published by John Whittaker in 1823, with full pages devoted to court personages in their ceremonial robes, drew large crowds. Mrs. Thorne's collection was unique because she had secured not only the important color plate books, but the original water colors from which the prints were made.

Narcissa hosted several afternoon teas for friends and members of the Print and Drawing Club in the Print Rooms of the Art Institute where they could view her collection, which was considered to be one of the most notable and impressive of its kind ever exhibited.

The Thorne Exhibit

"Whoever enjoys illustrated books should visit the Art Institute at the earliest possible moment but in any event not later than March 15th. Mrs. James Ward Thorne, who has the finest collection of color-plate books, original drawings for them, fore-edge paintings, panoramas and peep shows in the world, has made a selection of her most beautiful items, and sent them to the Print Rooms of the Art Institute."

Edited by Llewellyn Jones
Chicago Evening Post Literary Section
February 12, 1932

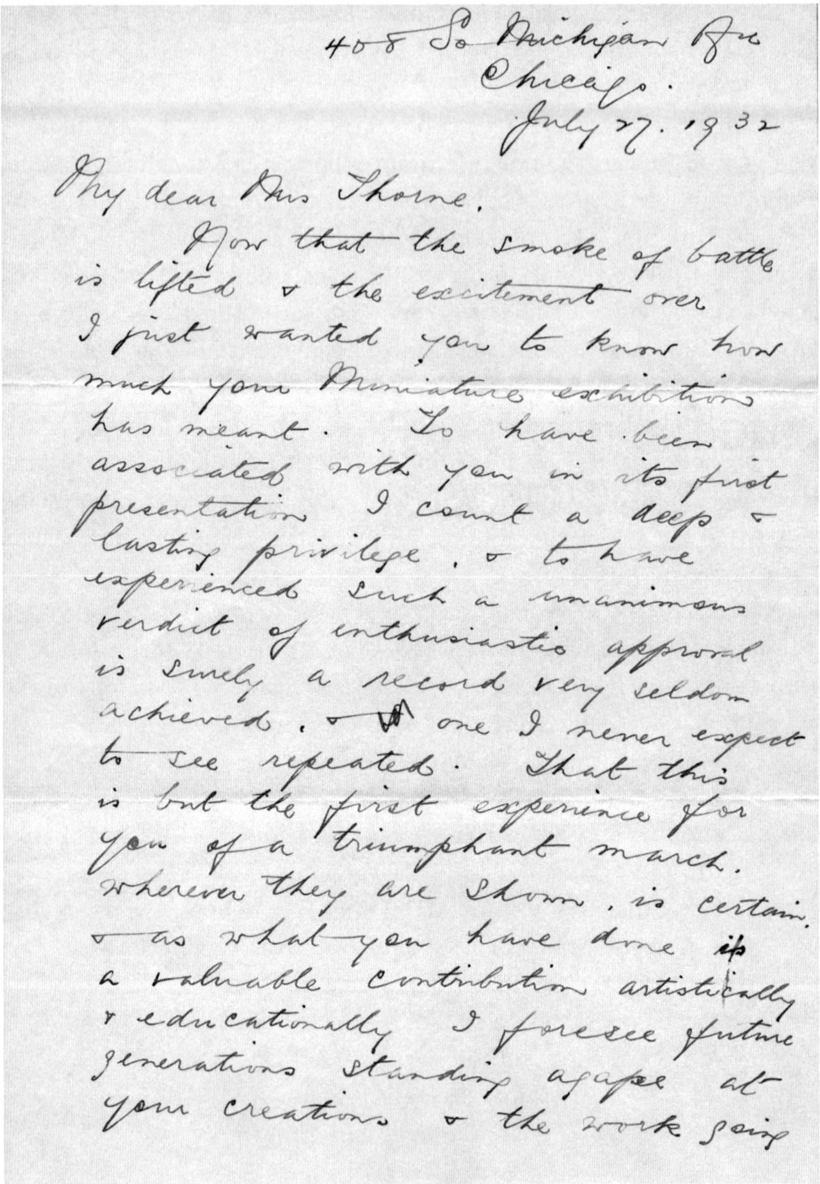

408 So Michigan Ave
Chicago.
July 27. 1932

My dear Mrs Thorne,

Now that the smoke of battle is lifted & the excitement over I just wanted you to know how much your Miniature exhibition has meant. To have been associated with you in its first presentation I count a deep & lasting privilege, & to have experienced such a unanimous verdict of enthusiastic approval is surely a record very seldom achieved, & one I never expect to see repeated. That this is but the first experience for you of a triumphant march wherever they are shown, is certain. & as what you have done is a valuable contribution artistically & educationally I foresee future generations standing agape at your creations & the work going

Letter from W. Russell Button of Ackermann Galleries where 12 miniature rooms were exhibited for the first time in June of 1932. (Courtesy of Anne Thorne Weaver)

Art Institute Has Good Show for Children
Two Exhibitions Possess Special Appeal

"There are two exhibitions at the Art Institute to which you should take your children. They will enjoy as much as you the delightful animals in the children's museum and the fascinating peep shows and illustrations of children in the Mrs. James Ward Thorne's collection on exhibit in the Print galleries."

Eleanor Jewett
Chicago Daily Tribune
February 12, 1932

The rare book and print show proved to be very popular, but Mrs. Thorne's friends eagerly awaited the unveiling of the much-talked about miniature rooms that had been her focus since December of 1931. Finally, in June of 1932, the first set of 12 rooms was completed and 10 were exhibited in the Ackermann Galleries located at 408 South Michigan Avenue to benefit the Architects Relief Fund at a time when so many architects were out of work and actively seeking commissions. More than 2,200 people visited the rooms with an entry fee of 25¢. A great deal of money was raised for draftsmen and architects who benefitted from the small admission fees and additional donations.

Visitors included Mrs. Woodrow Wilson and Mrs. J. Ogden Armour. After seeing the exquisite rooms, Mrs. Armour decided to reproduce in miniature some of the rooms in her home, Melody Farm, in Lake Forest.

Model Rooms by Mrs. Thorne to Be Shown
Lovely Miniatures Will Have Preview

"I predict there will be such a crush on Monday afternoon (opening preview), for everyone is so anxious to see those marvelous little rooms that all those who are invited will have to go another time to really see the rooms. No cursory examination would suffice for them. They are worth careful examination for each detail is perfect and the rooms are as lovely examples of period architecture and decoration as one could find anywhere."

Judith Cass
Chicago Daily Tribune
June 9, 1932

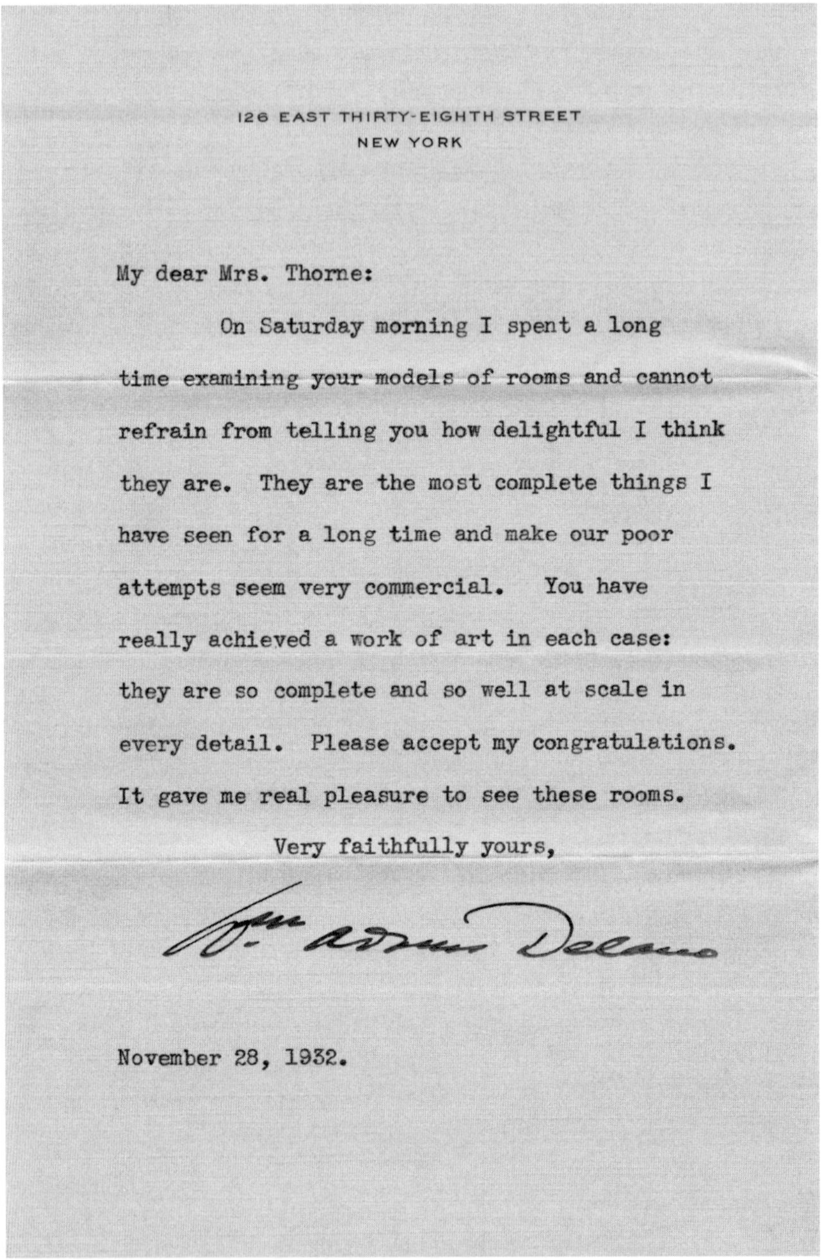

126 EAST THIRTY-EIGHTH STREET
NEW YORK

My dear Mrs. Thorne:

On Saturday morning I spent a long time examining your models of rooms and cannot refrain from telling you how delightful I think they are. They are the most complete things I have seen for a long time and make our poor attempts seem very commercial. You have really achieved a work of art in each case: they are so complete and so well at scale in every detail. Please accept my congratulations. It gave me real pleasure to see these rooms.

Very faithfully yours,

November 28, 1932.

Congratulatory letter from New York architect William Adams Delano of Delano & Aldrich Architects in 1932. (Courtesy of Anne Thorne Weaver)

The Women's Division of the Architects' Emergency Committee
invites you to an Exhibition of a
Collection of

MINIATURE PERIOD ROOMS

Designed and arranged by
MRS. JAMES WARD THORNE
at the
ACKERMANN GALLERIES
50 East 57th Street
New York

November first to thirtieth inclusive
Entire Proceeds for the
ARCHITECTS' EMERGENCY FUND

Admission 50 cents Daily, except Sunday, 9 a. m. to 6 p. m.

Invitation to attend miniature room exhibit at New York Ackermann Galleries in November of 1932. (Courtesy of Anne Thorne Weaver)

The exhibit was so successful that the women's division of the Architects Emergency Committee of New York asked Mrs. Thorne to lend the rooms to display for their own benefit to be held at Ackermann Galleries located at 50 East 57th Street. In November of 1932 the rooms traveled to New York for another successful showing.

If the Little People Could Come Out of the Hills They Would Feel Much at Home in Mrs. James Ward Thorne's Miniature Interiors.

"Mrs. Thorne has traveled 'everywhere,' and it was the appeal of the tiny which launched her on collecting all sorts of exquisite little art objects. Of late, when her luggage is opened before custom officials, they scratch their heads in bewilderment. How to appraise these multitudinous charming knick-knacks while Mr. Thorne looks on with amusement?"

Edith W. Powell
The New York Sun
November 1, 1932

Because of the enthusiasm over the rooms, Mrs. Thorne was asked to introduce the miniature rooms to the general public at the Century of Progress World's Fair held in Chicago in 1933–34.

The Fair illustrated the advances in technology, exhibiting everything new and modern. Unlike the classical architecture of the Columbian Exposition of 1893, this Fair told the story of the future.

It was the age of the electrical revolution with the Science Halls introducing all manner of inventions.

Reconstruction of quaint historical villages had been a part of expositions for years. Always popular, visitors flocked to the area to experience a different culture while eating the food, attending the musicals, and buying souvenirs. In May of 1933, the miniature rooms were installed and exhibited on the "Streets of Paris," but Mrs. Thorne was not pleased with the location. The Streets offered cabaret shows and peep shows, more in keeping with the red light district of the City of Lights. It was a district filled with risqué concessions and cafes where young women could find work. Mrs. Thorne remarked, "I blush to think how ill-chosen its location was in the Streets of Paris!"

After the excitement and work constructing and exhibiting the first 12 rooms at the Fair, the Thornes sailed to Europe in August of 1933, planned as a rest cure for Mrs. Thorne's tired nerves. She made a promise to herself and to her family to relax and to "stop this collecting!"— a phrase used often within her home. But when they reached London she immediately began visiting all museums that contained dollhouses and collections of miniature furniture.

She had heard of an antique dealer who specialized in miniatures from all over the world, and was determined to find him. A visit to Aspreys on Bond Street proved successful. One of the salesmen knew of the store and walked her to the antique shop. Inside were numerous treasures and she said, "It was utterly fascinating and my complete undoing."

As Mrs. Thorne was sorting through the miniatures, she explained to the saleswoman the type of items and scale she wanted. Immediately the saleswoman brought out the catalogue from the Century of Progress World's Fair, and told Mrs. Thorne she might be interested in attending to view the 12 miniature rooms on display!

Another young man browsing in the shop said he had seen the rooms in Chicago when they were first exhibited at Ackermann Galleries for the benefit of the Architects Relief Fund. After Mrs. Thorne confessed

To Mrs. Thorne's chagrin, in 1933 her first 12 rooms were displayed in the "Streets of Paris" exhibit at the Century of Progress. (*Courtesy of Lake County* (*IL*) *Discovery Museum, Curt Teich Postcard Archives*)

to being the American woman who designed the rooms, they shared a chuckle at the curious coincidence that had brought them together.

Her resolution to stop collecting soon became hopeless when Mrs. Thorne found the cabinet maker who had made many exquisite items for Queen Mary's dollhouse and for Sir Nevile Wilkinson, who owned and exhibited Titania's Palace. She commissioned the cabinet maker to design rooms from three different English country houses, and a large library that might be found in a London townhouse in Berkeley Square. Mrs. Thorne had a small globe of the world the size of a marble that she intended to have mounted as an ornament and placed in the library. The cabinet maker was intrigued with the globe, especially when he learned it had been purchased in a dime store in Chicago! He thought Queen Mary would be thrilled to receive one to add to her enormous collection of miniatures. When Mrs. Thorne returned to the United States she sent one to Queen Mary to add to her private collection housed in Buckingham Palace.

The Thornes continued their travels to Canterbury in southern England to visit a proprietress of a tiny, stuffy shop in the Close of the Cathedral. Mrs. Thorne said she felt a thrill of pleasure when she heard the jingle of the bell opening the door. At once the owner recognized her

French Breton Kitchen. The room contains tiny pieces of pottery, brass, and copper purchased in Brittany and Normandy. (Courtesy of Chicago History Museum)

from a previous visit, and they spent the afternoon speaking about miniatures as only born collectors can do. Mrs. Thorne shared photographs of the English Victorian Parlor which she had designed that contained the small Rockingham lamb that she had purchased from the owner. The proprietress was happy the lamb had been properly placed in the correct room since she became so attached to the miniatures that to her they were almost human! Mrs. Thorne purchased additional treasures at the shop before departing for Salisbury.

Near the Cathedral in Salisbury she found a shop that contained a collection of medallions which she purchased. They became the inspiration for the English Adam Dining Room.

In Exeter, Mrs. Thorne finally was able to visit Titania's Palace, on view to benefit a local children's charity. She was impressed with the marvelous treasures, but not the scale. "In the arrangement of the rooms, there is absolutely no attention paid to scale, and the most incongruous placing of articles destroys the charm of the general effect."

The Thornes continued their journey to the French countryside, visiting Brittany and Normandy to study the old houses and museums in order to design a French Breton Kitchen that Mrs. Thorne had dreamed about for so many years. At Mont St. Michel she found almost all the small furniture she needed—delicately carved cradles, beds, spinning wheels, etc. When she reached Quimper, a town that was reportedly noted for its miniatures, there were no pieces to be bought. Mrs. Thorne said she always adhered to one rule in her massive collecting: "When I see what I am looking for, I buy it then and there. Sometimes, I am wrong and find later that I could have done better. But, in most cases, I am glad that I have followed my instinct."

After weeks of traveling and collecting during the so-called "rest cure" trip, the Thornes had to purchase additional trunks before sailing home from France. When they landed at American Customs the officer and Mrs. Thorne knelt down on the dock beside the trunks while she tried to explain the "mental quirk which inspired her to buy such things." Finally, he said, "There is no precedent for this sort of thing. I give up. Let's call it so many pounds of brass, wood, and china." And they did!

After returning to Chicago, Mrs. Thorne organized the additional rooms she wanted to design. Work started in December of 1933 and she hired several out-of-work artisans to help construct 14 new rooms.

The French Breton Kitchen contained the small kitchen utensils found at Mont St. Michel. At the back of the room the cabinet was filled with china and other family treasures. She included a figure of a Breton woman, an idea she did not repeat in subsequent series, realizing the figures detracted from the overall authentic look of the room.

The English Dining Room was inspired by architect Robert Adam who worked out a new vocabulary of classical architecture. He was a brilliant ornamental designer who supervised the decoration and furnishings of his houses down to the last detail, "even the door locks!" He worked with the finest craftsmen of the day including Thomas Chippendale. His ceilings were famous, and Mrs. Thorne used his design for delicate plaster medallions to create her dining room.

The 14 additional rooms were completed on May 22, just four days before the Century of Progress World's Fair reopened in 1934. The rooms offered a selection of European and American Rooms dating from Jacobean 17th century to the modern 1920s.

Mrs. Thorne said, "It was a tremendous task, but a fascinating one and it gave so many people employment during last winter that I feel the development of my hobby has been well worthwhile."

Fortunately, the total of 26 rooms were displayed in the former Edison building located in the South Lagoon; a more acceptable location than the "Streets of Paris" in 1933. With all rooms housed in one building, they were labeled "Mrs. Thorne's Miniature Rooms."

Mrs. James Ward Thorne Will Exhibit Twenty-Six Miniature Rooms at Fair Fourteen New Interiors to be Added to Her Famous Collection and Housed in Own Building on Northerly Island

Chicago Tribune

May 1934

During the 1933–34 Fair, Mrs. Thorne was asked to give a number of speeches and the idea of a book presented itself. Hans Huth, furniture specialist and later Curator of Decorative Arts at the Art Institute of Chicago, offered suggestions of topics the public would be interested in knowing about. After asking four pages of questions in a letter addressed to Mrs. Thorne in March of 1933, Mr. Huth said it could be a small book in spite of all this information! The project must have seemed daunting because it was never realized.

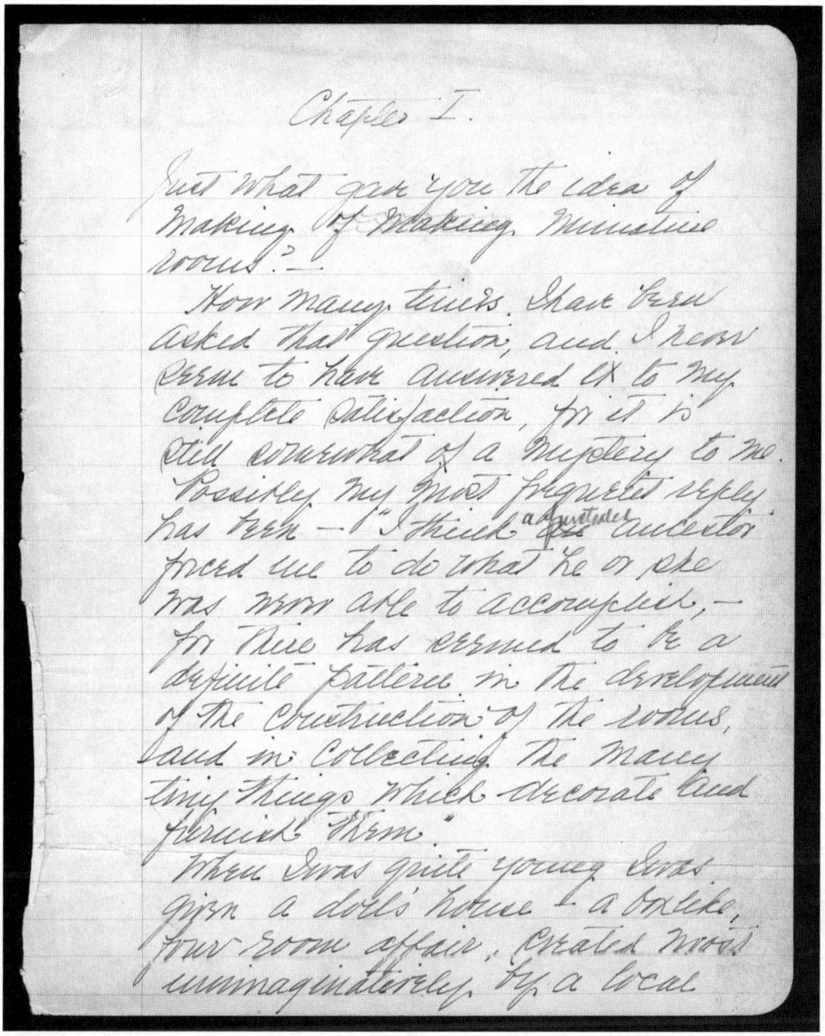

Chapter I.

Just what gave you the idea of making of making miniature rooms?—

How many times I have been asked that question, and I never seem to have answered it to my complete satisfaction, for it is still somewhat of a mystery to me. Possibly my most frequent reply has been—"I think a forgotten ancestor forced me to do what he or she was never able to accomplish,— for there has seemed to be a definite pattern in the development of the construction of the rooms, and in collecting the many tiny things which decorate and furnish them."

When I was quite young I was given a doll's house — a boxlike, four-room affair, created most unimaginatively by a local

Chapter One of a proposed book about the Thorne Miniature Rooms that was never realized. (Courtesy of Anne Thorne Weaver)

Anne Thorne Weaver's favorite picture of her grandmother relaxing in the garden of her Santa Barbara home. (Courtesy of Anne Thorne Weaver)

CHAPTER 5

A HOBBY BECOMES A MANIA

"Who contributed more to the interest of the Art Institute of Chicago than Mrs. James Ward Thorne with her exquisite rooms? They are perfect in detail. Chicago has much to be proud of in her women who can stand beside the truly great men of this city."

Strange to Say: Recollections of Persons and Events in New Orleans and Chicago by Edith Ogden Harrison (Mrs. Carter Harrison, Jr.)

After the Century of Progress World's Fair, the miniature rooms were on display at the Chicago Historical Society from 1934–37. They continued to be a popular exhibit and drew large crowds. Mrs. Thorne decided to move her inventory of miniatures to a large studio to concentrate on designing additional rooms.

After finding a commodious workshop she began a search for artisans to do the work. "Having had experience in model making myself, I realized that I would have to employ craftsmen of great ability and skill to accomplish my purpose. Of course, my first object was to obtain the services of a fine draftsman to draw all the plans. After trying two ineffectual young men, I was ready to give up my project, but the third applicant not only understood my aim, but had the same feeling for scale and we worked together happily for 12 years. He drew the interior designs of all the rooms, the furniture, china and glass, keeping the most accurate scale of one inch to one foot.

"We had excellent books of reference, drawings and photographs for his use. I was extremely lucky to find a remarkable model maker (this is a gift) and his was perfect in every detail. He and his assistants were geniuses in their line of work and always seemed to find a way out of any difficulty. An artist of real talent had done some work for me at one time and he was persuaded to join our group and do the painting of the rooms.

Every inch of the woodwork, floors, and paneling was grained to scale and the wallpaper copied from the large designs in the original rooms."

The second set of 31 rooms was European, dating from the Gothic 14th Century Catholic Church to the 20th century "modern" room. Most dated from the 18th century because Mrs. Thorne felt that interior design reached its zenith during that time period.

In the first set of rooms she had used the shells (or rooms) as backgrounds or sets to contain her large collection of miniatures which she had been gathering for years. In her European set she was determined to create architecturally precise rooms and the furnishings, in most instances, were made for the room.

"In this set of rooms I have endeavored to show the chronological evolution of English and French rooms from the Gothic period to present day. Many of these are reproductions of noted rooms, copied as accurately as possible, while others are more or less composite types, but in all of these models I have tried to give students of architecture a clear idea of the outstanding characteristics of each period."

Mrs. Thorne started her European adventure designing several rooms from familiar English Treasure Houses.

KNOLE HOUSE

When the Thornes traveled to England, they visited Knole in Kent, once the palace of the archbishop of Canterbury, then a royal palace. Knole came to its fulfillment as the Sackville-West family home deeded to them by Queen Elizabeth I in 1566. Covering five acres and containing 365 rooms, it is more of a medieval village than a house. The interior is richly decorated, as Elizabethan and Jacobean interiors always were, with elaborate carvings and plasterwork, long galleries and grand staircases.

Mrs. Thorne reproduced a bedroom from Knole with its elaborate walnut paneled walls, window recess, and mantel. The needlepoint picture to the right of the fireplace and the tapestry over the Court cupboard were made in Vienna. But the tapestries presented problems. In Paris, Mrs. Thorne bought women's handbags and vanity cases of many different sizes and shapes made of needlework. She cut them for chair seats, couches, pictures, and tapestry hangings.

"These I had to tear apart to use in my work and this method of destruction was so ruinous that I realized I must trace the origin of this work and buy the pieces unmounted. Vienna was to be my destination and I started at once on the quest. My first day in Vienna would have

Knole House located in Kent, England. Inspiration for the English Bedchamber of the Jacobean or Stuart Period, 1603–88. (Courtesy of Cornell University Library)

discouraged the most courageous soul. I could speak Italian and French, but not one word of German could I utter or understand. Not even the owner of the shop could help me. I was sitting in blank despair when the door opened and in walked an acquaintance I had not seen for years. She proved to be quite a friend of the proprietress of the shop and she spoke excellent German. From that moment on my troubles were no more. Messengers were sent out all over Vienna to get the pieces of petit point which were being made in the homes of many families. The next day we went back to find every size, shape and design that I wanted for the English and French rooms. They were unmounted and worked on the finest of net, in perfect shape for me to use. My joy was profound and my guardian angel was duly thanked."

The silver pieces on the dressing table in the Knole Bedroom (English Bedchamber), as well as the candlesticks, were made in England and purchased at Arthur Punt's, a London store she frequented.

The view through the window illustrates Mrs. Thorne's love of gardens. This garden was largely created by Vita Sackville-West who had a profound knowledge of gardening. Although an only child, Vita was unable to inherit Knole because of gender (her uncle inherited the estate). In 1930, after she married Harold Nicholson, they bought Sissinghurst Castle, also located in Kent, and together created the famous Sissinghurst Gardens.

(See E-2: English Bedchamber of the Jacobean or Stuart Period, 1603–88 at the Art Institute of Chicago.)

Belton House in Lincolnshire, England. Inspiration for the English Drawing Room of the late Jacobean Period, 1680–1702. (Courtesy of University of California Libraries)

BELTON HOUSE

Mr. And Mrs. Thorne also visited Belton House, another English country house that was used as the setting for an earlier version of *Pride and Prejudice* by Jane Austen. Originally owned by the Brownlow Family of Lincolnshire, it was built in 1684 and was noted for its famous woodcarving by Grinling Gibbons, the finest wood-carver of his day. It is an excellent example of the collaboration of the architect Christopher Wren and the carver Gibbons at their best. Mrs. Thorne was impressed with the library carvings, ceilings, and moldings of fruits and flowers as well as the paneled and marble-floored hall.

There is a particularly amusing story about tea-drinking at Belton in the late 17th century when it was considered an expensive and exclusive custom. A pound of tea in the 1720s cost about one hundred times as much as it would at today's values, reason enough to keep the tea caddies locked. One afternoon Sir John Brownlow's five daughters were caught hosting a tea party on the first floor. They heard their Mother's footsteps approaching, and in a panic, threw the tea set out the window!

For Mrs. Thorne's Belton-inspired room, she purchased a rug found in an antique shop in Paris. It was lined with heavy damask and had been used by the owner to put under a kerosene lamp! After a thorough cleaning, it developed into a remarkable reproduction of an oriental rug.

Belton House carving in the Great Hall by Grinling Gibbons. (Courtesy of University of California Libraries)

She purchased the secretary, the cabinet and clock in the London Shop of Arthur Punt, the only source she ever divulged.

(*See E-4: English Drawing Room of the Late Jacobean Period, 1680–1702 at the Art Institute.*)

Many of the paintings that appear in the Thorne Rooms were painted by well-known artists—Léger, Ozenfant and Survage.

Double Cube Room at Wilton House. Along with the Single Cube Room it was the inspiration for the English Reception Room of the Jacobean Period, 1625–55. (Courtesy of University of California Libraries)

WILTON HOUSE

The land on which Wilton House was built was taken from an ancient monastery and given to Sir William Herbert by Henry VIII in 1544. It is the only surviving country house attributed to the master Palladian architect, Inigo Jones, who had brought new ideas from Italy. The white woodwork, gold carved swags, damask walls, and colorful ceilings were a radical change from the dark and rather dreary decorating of the past. The Double Cube Room designed by Inigo Jones and his son-in-law, John Gibbs, is 60 feet long with richly carved walls designed to set off magnificent portraits by van Dyck. The Colonnade, or Single Cube Room, exhibits the paintings of Joshua Reynolds and decorative furniture by William Kent.

For her room inspired by Wilton House, Mrs. Thorne combined features of both the Single and Double Cube Rooms of Wilton: the tables resemble originals by William Kent and copies of the van Dyck portraits were created for the room. The black and white tiled floor is a copy from the Queen's House in Greenwich, another Inigo Jones design.

Wilton's reputation as a meeting place for brilliant minds was enhanced when Shakespeare's company performed *As You Like It* for James I in

West facade of Wilton House in Salisbury, England, designed by Inigo Jones. (Courtesy of Cornell University Library)

1603. London theaters had been forced to close because of an outbreak of the plague. During World War II, Wilton House was the headquarters of the Southern Command and the Double Cube Room was the secret operations center for planning the Normandy invasion.

(See E-3: English Reception Room of the Jacobean Period, 1625–55 at the Art Institute. It is also shown on the back cover of this book.)

COTSWOLD COTTAGES

The Queen Anne Cottage is similar to Anne Hathaway's (married to William Shakespeare) home near Stratford-upon-Avon and typical of the Cotswold Cottages in the area. The furniture is of dark oak, and the chairs made of yew, a tough wood which lent itself readily to the reed construction of the Windsor chair. The oak dresser occupied a place of importance. This is where the average housewife displayed her treasures of pewter, brass, and china. The high-back settle (bench) near the fireplace kept the chill off one's back during the cold winter.

There is an interesting story about the birdhouse hanging in front of the window overlooking the flower garden and thatched roofs of neighboring cottages. On occasion, Mrs. Thorne admitted to having been an "abandoned vandal," especially when she deliberately took the most "devastatingly cute birdhouse I ever saw from the top of my grandmother's favorite music box. The garden of the Cotswold cottage was waiting for that birdhouse, and I quickly broke its under-pinnings, took it to my shop, and placed it where I was certain it belonged!"

When interviewed on February 26, 1946 by the *Toronto Daily Star* Mrs. Thorne said she preferred the rooms in which she could sit and rest her feet. The English Cottage Kitchen was one of her favorites.

(*See E-5: English Cottage Kitchen of the Queen Anne Period, 1702–14 at the Art Institute.*)

THE ENGLISH DRAWING ROOM

Mrs. Thorne's English Drawing Room of the Victorian Period is designed in the Gothic style so popular in England in 1850, and incorporates a wide range of the revival styles of Baroque, Rococo and Chippendale. The walls are pale lettuce green with white Gothic scroll and woodwork. The carpet is of tomato red, and the curtains are the same shade of red in satin with gold fringe. All the furniture is copied from pieces of the period and the tiny ornaments had been part of her cherished collection for years. A copy of the souvenir coronation book with pictures of the royal family rests on the pedestal table in the front left foreground of the room. Portraits of Queen Victoria and Prince Albert hang in the back of the room and prints of Osborne and Balmoral Castles hang on either side of the fireplace. Although the étagère and pedestal table are from an earlier period, Mrs. Thorne intentionally incorporated these pieces into the room.

"In furnishing these rooms of other centuries, one must blend imagination with our modern conception of what they looked like when they were occupied by living men and women. As we look upon the empty shells which are left to us, they seem very lifeless and austere. But, after all, they were homes and must have home-like atmospheres."

(*See E-14: English Drawing Room of the Victorian Period, 1840–70 at the Art Institute of Chicago.*)

THE 20TH CENTURY ENGLISH DRAWING ROOM

The English Drawing Room of the Modern Period was an interesting deviation for Mrs. Thorne. No time travel was necessary to create the drawing room of the modern period. She blended the scroll and shell design of the Rococo ornament with the glass, chromium and some dark mahogany pieces suggestive of the Georgian influence. The portrait over the mantel is of King Edward VIII wearing his royal robes, and the royal blue velvet curtains reflect the king's wardrobe. Lying on the white sofa is an accurate replica of *English Country Life* magazine which can be read with a magnifying glass. The statue on the glass pedestal is of a modern Mona Lisa, reportedly Wallis Simpson, future wife of King Edward VIII.

Mrs. Thorne's room might have been inspired by the famous English interior designer Syrie Maugham who is given credit for designing the first all-white room. During the 1920s and 1930s Maugham opened a shop in London which became so lucrative that additional shops were opened in New York and Chicago. Although Mrs. Thorne did not give credit to Syrie Maugham, she did admire Maugham's rooms which mixed the fashionable Rococo style, modern furniture, and touches of antiques.

(*See E-15: English Drawing Room of the Modern Period, 1930s at the Art Institute.*)

LOUIS XIV

Mrs. Thorne decided to devote two rooms to the period of Louis XIV, the Sun King. It was a time of opulence with baroque furniture set in formal arrangements in rooms with high ceilings, tall windows, and niches holding statues. The French Salon, where Louis XIV entertained the nobles, illustrates the decorative designs of elaborately carved furniture and ceilings in the architectural style of Jean Le Pautre, a noted architect of the time. The color scheme is also characteristic—light green walls and darker green marble pilasters with gilded moldings. (Originally the decorative details of ceiling, moldings, etc. had to be done by hand, using regular plaster. Today rubber and plastic molds are used.)

The portrait of Louis XIV wearing robes of state hanging over the fireplace is a copy of Rigaud's painting in the Louvre. Louis XIV used the letter "L" wherever he could in the decoration as well as a head surrounded by rays of the sun, the emblem of the Sun King. During this time Chinese porcelain was introduced and it became the vogue to collect it if you could afford the then enormous prices. The table in the center of the room is a copy of a piece from the Louvre and the two wonderfully tooled books have text and illustrations.

(*See E-18: French Salon of the Louis XIV Period 1660–1700 at the Art Institute.*)

Georgian Library donated to Victoria & Albert Museum in London in 1937. (Courtesy of Anne Thorne Weaver)

LOUIS XV

The French Boudoir was inspired by Madame de Pompadour's influence on the arts and King Louis XV's desire for more luxurious and comfortable surroundings. The chalk white walls and lighter tones of woods, draperies, and fabrics reflect the charming taste of his mistress, Madame de Pompadour.

The chaise-lounge in the foreground and bergère chair accommodated the wide skirts and stiff brocades worn by members of the court.

The cabriole, or curved leg, reached its most popular development during this period, and is considered the distinguishing characteristic of Louis XV style. On the back wall is a very fine piece of petit point, imitating a tapestry. This was a lucky find in an antique shop in the Latin Quarter of Paris. Mrs. Thorne never revealed the names of her favorite small (and usually hidden) antique and curiosity shops in Paris, Rome, Florence, Vienna, etc. The only source of treasures that she shared with the public was Arthur Punt's shop in London.

(See E-21: French Boudoir of the Louis XV Period, 1740–60 at the Art Institute.)

GEORGIAN INFLUENCE

In 1935 while Mrs. Thorne was busy working seven days a week to complete the European Rooms, she received a request from Queen Mary of England to construct a copy of a miniature room to be placed in the Victoria & Albert Museum in London. Queen Mary, whose interest in miniatures was well-known, selected the Georgian Library first shown to the general public at the Century of Progress World's Fair in 1933–34.

The room, in the style of architects William Kent and James Gibbs, could not be reproduced exactly because some of the tiny furnishings and ornaments of the original room were antiques and could not be copied even by Mrs. Thorne's talented artisans and craftsmen. She decided to make some alterations to the room she would design for Queen Mary.

The doorway was reproduced from an example of an 18th century house in Hatton Gardens, London. William Kent mantel, Chippendale furniture, Gainsborough paintings, a Coromandel screen made in China, and a needlepoint Georgian designed rug by the Needlepoint and Textile Guild of the Art Institute contributed to the authenticity of the time period. Beside the back right window stands an architect's table with a painting in process, another example of Mrs. Thorne's insistence on creating a realistic home atmosphere.

Most of the furniture for the room was made by Mr. A. Reeves, a British ex-policeman who started his career working with Alfred Punt in London. Mrs. Thorne had seen examples of Mr. Reeves's detailed work and hired him to produce much of the furniture for the European Rooms. At 6′ 2″ tall with enormous hands, it seemed inconceivable, but Reeves was able to carve the tiny pieces with absolute precision.

Upon completion of the room in early 1937, visitors to the Chicago Historical Society had the rare opportunity to view the gift designed for Queen Mary. The room was obviously a favorite of Mrs. Thorne's because she decided to create a similar English Drawing Room from the early Georgian period as part of her set of European Rooms. The London townhouse at 22 Hatton Gardens was the inspiration once again, and furniture throughout the room was copied from pieces in the Victoria & Albert Museum. The ceiling and fireplace were altered, but the Chinese Coromandel screen, architect's table, needlepoint rug by the Textile and Needlepoint Guild, and a Gainsborough painting remained the same.

(*See E-7: English Drawing Room of the Early Georgian Period, 1730s at the Art Institute.*)

The Thornes intended to travel to London for the coronation of Edward VIII to be held in May of 1937 and bring the Georgian miniature room with them. They carefully packed it for the trans-Atlantic crossing, but attended the coronation of a different king, that of George VI. In December of 1936, King Edward VIII abdicated the throne to marry the American divorcée, Wallis Simpson, a scandal that left the Royal family reeling!

Mrs. Thorne wrote a fascinating paper about her trip to London to attend George VI's coronation on May 12, 1937. Here are some highlights:

> "The Coronation ceremony really began on the night of May 11th. All that day, on the London streets, in the pouring rain, crowds were forming—joyous, exuberant crowds, singing, laughing, joking—no one objectionable.
>
> "We were occupying a house on Sloane Court not far from Westminster Abbey, ordinarily such a peaceful spot that I had been awakened in the morning by song birds in our garden. On this memorable night, the whole neighborhood was pandemonium. By 10 p.m. our little street was solidly blocked with motor cars, all from outlying districts of the city. The owners settled down inside their cars to relax for a few hours before starting for the particular gate which their ticket designated. There were huge gates built across a certain number of the major London streets through which the procession was to pass. Then all other streets were blocked off, and the night before the coronation all the gates were closed to vehicle traffic.
>
> "The public was warned that at 6 a.m. sharp the morning of May 12th these gates would also be closed to pedestrians and the line of march would be cleared. It was get there before six or no admittance. Needless to say, no one who really wanted to see the festivities took the slightest chance of being late.
>
> "At just ten minutes before six we drew up at the gate of Westminster Bridge and from there we walked. I shall never forget that misty river, the dark towers of the abbey, standing out against a gray sky, the colorful grandstands stretching endlessly down the embankment, and the surging mass of hurrying, scurrying people.

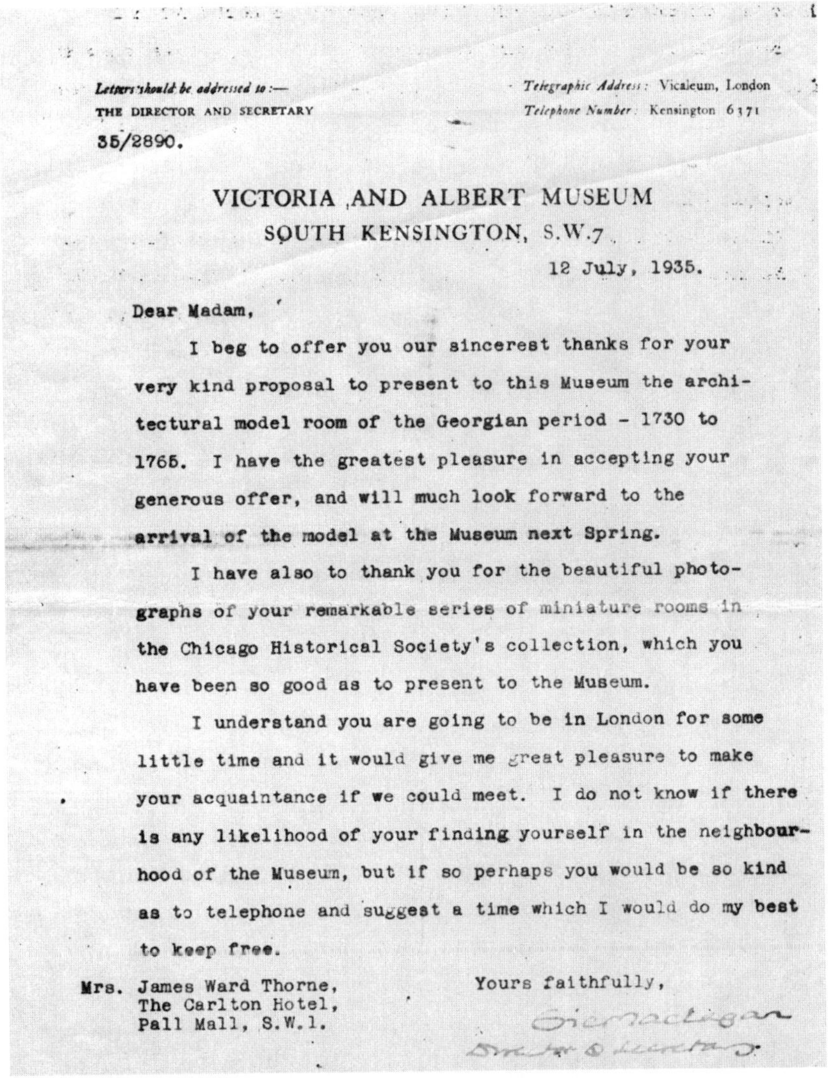

Letters should be addressed to:—
THE DIRECTOR AND SECRETARY

Telegraphic Address: Vicaleum, London
Telephone Number: Kensington 6371

35/2890.

VICTORIA AND ALBERT MUSEUM
SOUTH KENSINGTON, S.W.7

12 July, 1935.

Dear Madam,

I beg to offer you our sincerest thanks for your very kind proposal to present to this Museum the architectural model room of the Georgian period - 1730 to 1765. I have the greatest pleasure in accepting your generous offer, and will much look forward to the arrival of the model at the Museum next Spring.

I have also to thank you for the beautiful photographs of your remarkable series of miniature rooms in the Chicago Historical Society's collection, which you have been so good as to present to the Museum.

I understand you are going to be in London for some little time and it would give me great pleasure to make your acquaintance if we could meet. I do not know if there is any likelihood of your finding yourself in the neighbourhood of the Museum, but if so perhaps you would be so kind as to telephone and suggest a time which I would do my best to keep free.

Mrs. James Ward Thorne,
The Carlton Hotel,
Pall Mall, S.W.1.

Yours faithfully,

Letter from the Victoria and Albert Museum in London thanking Mrs. Thorne for her donation of a miniature model room of the Georgian Period, 1730–1765. (Courtesy of Anne Thorne Weaver)

"We were most fortunate in our seats, for our stand nestled close to the abbey where we saw the procession coming toward us to Westminster and leaving to return to Buckingham Palace. As we took our places, and looked out over the line of march, it seemed as though the entire population of England had gathered in the streets of London. During the past twenty-four hours, men, women and children had taken their places along the curb where they had slept in the rain.

"A break in the procession and then came the Duchess of Kent and the Duchess of Gloucester in a royal coach, looking radiantly beautiful in their low cut gowns of white satin covered with pearl embroidery, their colorful decorations, velvet trains, and oh! such jewels!

"The Princess Royal with her two nieces, Princess Elizabeth and Princess Margaret Rose came next. The way England loves those two little princesses is really most appealing. The applause and cheers were deafening when their heads bobbed at the windows of their coach, and when they waved their hands graciously, the crowds burst into applause.

"Queen Mary is to all Englishmen, still the great Queen of England. Of late she has gone through so much mental and emotional strain, and yet she holds her head high, looks at the world with those clear blue eyes, and is the very embodiment of all that is royal. The nation had a clear sympathy for her on this particular day, and they showed it by the most deafening cheers that thousands upon thousands of throats could shout.

"As I saw her coach approach I watched the people about me on the grandstand. Many were wiping their eyes as I was. Queen Mary and Queen Maud of Norway drove together in a resplendent gold coach. They were wonderfully regal looking women. Certainly after seeing these magnificent costumes, the tiaras and other jewels of the rarest beauty you realize that, very definitely, clothes do make the woman!

"After the two Queens descended at the abbey, there was a lull—that breathless lull of intense excitement. The eight horses, known as the Windsor greys came into view; the postilions and attendants in red and white uniforms and the horses in gorgeous red trappings. They were drawing the glass coach in which sat the King and Queen. Those two

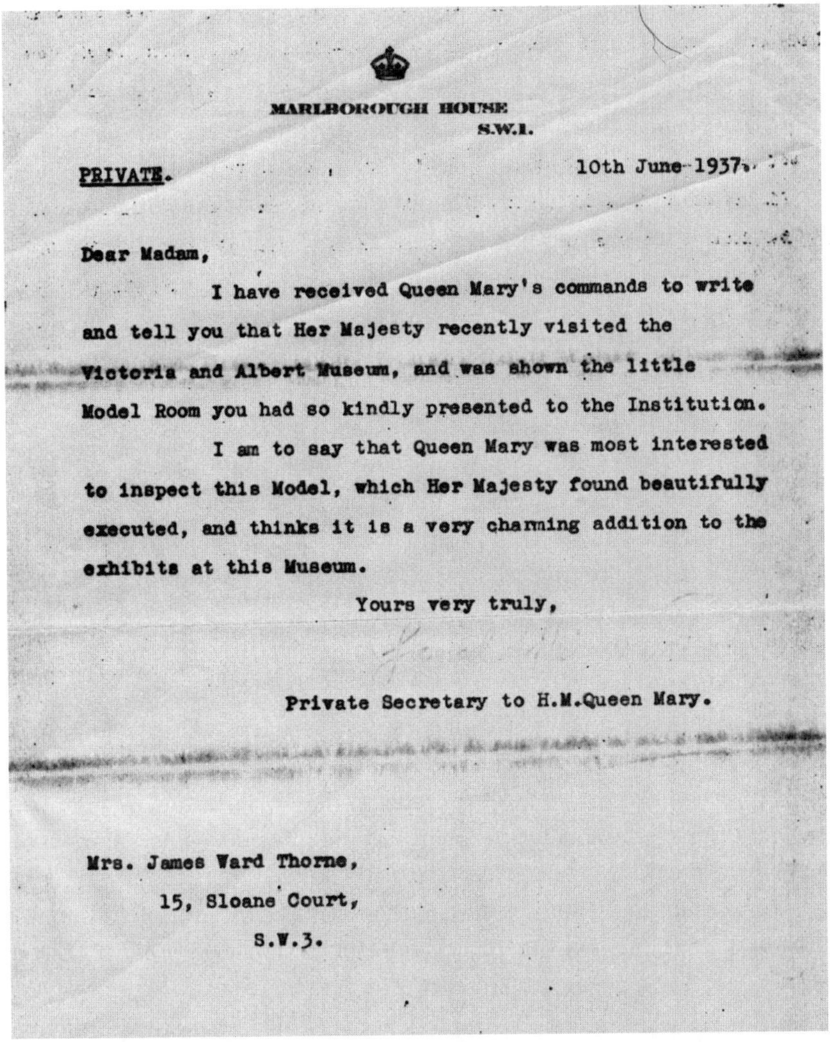

MARLBOROUGH HOUSE
S.W.1.

PRIVATE. 10th June 1937.

Dear Madam,

I have received Queen Mary's commands to write and tell you that Her Majesty recently visited the Victoria and Albert Museum, and was shown the little Model Room you had so kindly presented to the Institution.

I am to say that Queen Mary was most interested to inspect this Model, which Her Majesty found beautifully executed, and thinks it is a very charming addition to the exhibits at this Museum.

Yours very truly,

Private Secretary to H.M.Queen Mary.

Mrs. James Ward Thorne,
15, Sloane Court,
S.W.3.

In June of 1937 Queen Mary's personal secretary was "commanded" to write a note to Mrs. Thorne thanking her for the donation of the miniature Georgian period room. (Courtesy of Anne Thorne Weaver) figures will always be indelibly impressed upon my mind. The King's face was so drawn, you saw by the set of his jaw that his teeth were tight together. Yet his expression was spiritually beautiful. I said to myself, 'if there is to be another King of England, then he is the right King. He will take his duties seriously and earnestly uphold the dignity of his position.' Queen Elizabeth was very white, but calm and gracious. Her manner is spontaneous and natural. As she sat beside the King, she seemed to give him her strength for twice I saw him turn his head ever so slightly to speak to her. It was an exquisitely loving gesture. The crowd went quite mad over their sovereigns, and they were given a glorious welcome."

After King George VI's coronation, Mrs. Thorne presented the miniature Georgian library room to the Victoria & Albert Museum, and offered to pay for the installation. They politely refused because the case for the model could be made on location in their own workshop. The Victoria & Albert assured Mrs. Thorne that Queen Mary was very pleased with the gift.

The trip home on the *SS Normandie* was filled with relaxing days resting on the ship's deck chairs. This was the perfect opportunity for Mrs. Thorne to return to her needlework. She was working on an especially interesting project for her granddaughter, Anne—a needlepoint of Mickey Mouse to be used to cover a chair seat.

The project had begun with a request from Mrs. Potter Palmer II who wanted to present her granddaughter, Rose, with a chair covered with her favorite cartoon character. The Needlework Guild of the Art Institute drew the mouse, and Mrs. Thorne thought it would also make a wonderful gift for her granddaughter.

One day while Mrs. Thorne was working diligently to complete the needlepoint during her days at sea she noticed a couple had stopped and were staring at her work. Looking up, she was quite surprised to see Walt Disney and his wife! She hastened to explain that the Needlework Guild of the Chicago Art Institute had unthinkingly infringed upon his copyright.

Disney said because he had studied at the Art Institute he had a soft spot in his heart for it so he would forget the infringement, a gesture that was appreciated by Mrs. Thorne and the Guild.

A *Chicago Tribune* article of 1937 said the Needlework Guild will make no more!

The year 1937 proved to be auspicious for Mrs. Thorne not only for her exciting trip to England to attend George VI's coronation and donation of a miniature room to the Victoria & Albert Museum, but in addition, a serendipitous meeting that changed her life.

A detailed article about her miniature rooms appeared in the November 29th issue of *Life* magazine, and her reputation as an accomplished miniaturist spread across the United States and internationally. The historical rooms offering a comprehensive record of mankind's accomplishments attracted the attention of a local Chicago artisan, Eugene Kupjack.

After reading the article, Kupjack noticed that the rooms contained no cane furniture. He decided, as a master craftsman, he might be able to accomplish the task of constructing a miniature cane stool. He was able to complete the task, and sent Mrs. Thorne the stool as well as a plate and goblet made out of lucite.

Eugene Kupjack had attended classes at the Art Institute of Chicago for over 10 years, beginning at age eight! He attended Crane College and had aspirations to become a set designer for Hollywood. Kupjack was hired immediately at the age of 25 and spent almost 30 years on and off working for Mrs. Thorne as her most valued craftsman.

During the winter of 1937–38 the European Rooms were on exhibit at the Chicago Historical Society and the Art Institute of Chicago. The interest from adults and children was overwhelming, but Mrs. Thorne suspected the adults enjoyed them more because of the pleasure associated with viewing a work of art and the fun of entering an *Alice in Wonderland* world.

The directors of the Golden Gate Exposition requested that the Thorne Rooms be exhibited in San Francisco in 1939, and they became one of the most successful features of the Fair.

Because of the delicate and fragile nature of the rooms, Mrs. Thorne traveled to San Francisco with her sister, Lydia Swift, to supervise the installation in an airplane hangar at the south end of Treasure Island. They were an immediate success with over 1,000,000 visitors waiting in lines for 30 minutes or more.

The *Berkeley Gazette* reported that the Broadway and Hollywood stars voted the Thorne Rooms as the most interesting exhibit in the Fine and Decorative Arts Building.

Walt Disney attended the Exposition, visited the Thorne Rooms, and was inspired to start collecting miniatures during his travels to Europe. Actress Helen Hayes visited the Thorne Rooms numerous times and said,

> "They are like a stage setting. The remarkable fidelity is unique. I have never seen anything like them in my whole life."
>
> *Santa Rosa News*
> *August 1, 1939*

Wanted: Housemaid Not Afraid of Work

> "Mrs. Blanche Sudlow, on staff of the Chicago Historical Society traveled to San Francisco to clean the Thorne Rooms with tiny brushes and cloths."
>
> *San Francisco Chronicle*
> *August 12, 1939*

> "New signs were posted yesterday around the Thorne Rooms warning that the glass windows are real. A gentleman visitor leaned forward and tumbled a glass pane right into the miniature Georgian Room. Neither was seriously injured."
>
> *San Francisco Examiner*
> *April 7, 1939*

The Thorne Rooms continued their travels to New York in 1940 for the World's Fair. Again they were a success and began traveling throughout the art museums of the east coast, beginning with the Boston Museum of Fine Arts.

The European Rooms were completed and enthusiastically received by experts in the field. Why not bask in the glory? Not Mrs. Thorne. She wanted to continue with the untold American story.

THE ART INSTITUTE OF CHICAGO

POTTER PALMER, *President* CHARLES H. WORCESTER, *Honorary President* WALTER B. SMITH, *Treasurer*
ROBERT ALLERTON, *Vice-President* PERCY B. ECKHART, *Vice-President* CHAUNCEY McCORMICK, *Vice-President* RUSSELL TYSON, *Vice-President*
DANIEL CATTON RICH, *Director of Fine Arts* CHARLES H. BURKHOLDER, *Director of Finance and Operation* CHARLES FABENS KELLEY, *Assistant Director*

TELEPHONE CENTRAL 7080

November 29, 1938

My dear Mrs. Thorne:

In summing up the activities of the Art Institute for the year, the Trustees wish to thank you for your very generous contribution in making the Exhibit of Miniature Rooms possible. It was one of the most successful shows we have had, both from the standpoint of public interest and of attendance, and it will be long remembered.

The energy and devotion which you contributed, and the financial assistance you gave in getting the project started are deeply appreciated.

Very sincerely yours,

President

Mrs. James Ward Thorne
1500 Lake Shore Drive
Chicago, Illinois

1938 thank you letter from Potter Palmer II to Mrs. Thorne. (Courtesy of Anne Thorne Weaver)

Mrs. Thorne in her studio. (Courtesy of Anne Thorne Weaver)

CHAPTER 6

THE AMERICAN STORY

"Mrs. Thorne must be in the grip of a possessive hobby."
Minneapolis Star Journal
January 18, 1944

By 1939 Mrs. Thorne's staff of workers had perfected their individual skills and assignments in miniature making. They ran a well-oiled machine with artisans performing individual duties. Several craftsmen continuously experimented with miniatures, taking drawings home and returning with exquisite furniture and light fixtures which their clever fingers had produced.

Her team of experts included master carver Alfons Weber, who had worked for Marshall Field's as a window designer. Claus O. Brandell not only carved miniature furniture, but invented tools to make the task easier. When Eugene Kupjack joined the workforce he recommended his cousin, Lee Meisinger, to make the needlepoint rugs. Meisinger took lessons from the Needlework and Textile Guild of the Art Institute, which had provided immeasurable help to Mrs. Thorne in the past. Mrs. Thorne designed many of the rugs that were executed by Meisinger.

The new American venture consisted of 37 rooms from New England, the Middle Atlantic States, and the South, with a few examples from the West. The series illustrated a survey in chronological order of domestic interiors from the 17th century until 1940.

In the earlier rooms Mrs. Thorne had utilized many items from her own collection as well as miniatures she had purchased abroad. For the new series much of the furniture had to be made to scale. Reproductions of individual pieces were based on research. The furniture was by no means all American as many pieces in 18th century New England and Southern coastal area homes contained furniture imported from England.

From 1937 until 1940 Mrs. Thorne often worked seven days a week, creating, for the most part, reproductions or reconstructions of historic homes. Poring over research books, making blueprints of each room, she efficiently oversaw every detail while working on several rooms at the same time. She continued to upholster furniture and make curtains for the rooms, which she said, "was the most difficult millinery work."

While Mrs. Thorne was researching the American Rooms she wanted to visit a particular New England home. The owners refused her permission to visit so she went to the backyard, stuck her head through an opened window and memorized the interior!

THE MASSACHUSETTS DINING ROOM

This 1795 room was inspired by the Harrison Gray Otis house designed by architect Charles Bulfinch. Located in Boston's West End neighborhood, the Massachusetts Dining Room is reminiscent of English architect/decorator Robert Adam's style. The ornamentation of the mantel and above the doors, woodwork painted in shades of Wedgewood green, and Hepplewhite furniture were fashionable at the height of Adam's fame. Much of the furniture in this room is copied from English pieces because Otis, as well as other wealthy New England families during the 18th century, imported their furniture from England.

The wooden urns on either side of the sideboard contained slots to hold knives. Originally the knife boxes had slanted tops, but later in the century Adam used the urns as decorative pieces. The silver bowl on the sideboard bears the hallmark of a famous English silversmith.

Mrs. Thorne was often creative in finding items to use for specific purposes. Pieces of jewelry, typically earrings, were often used as wall sconces. In the Otis-inspired room she used actual Wedgewood buttons from her collection for the sconces above the fireplace. The Georgian needlework rug was a copy of an original from the Art Institute of Chicago. The Massachusetts Dining Room offers another example of excellent lighting techniques to simulate sunshine streaming in the square-paned windows, offering a view of the Georgian houses in the neighborhood. Today the Harrison Gray Otis house in Boston, located at the foot of Beacon Hill, is open to the public and definitely worth a visit.

(*See A10: Massachusetts Dining Room, 1795 at the Art Institute.*)

THE CAPE COD LIVING ROOM

As a less sophisticated room designed for a seafaring family from the Massachusetts coastal region, the Cape Cod Living Room from 1750–1850 was favored by Mrs. Thorne because it was a good place to rest your feet. The cozy room with a nautical theme contains a butterfly table, hoop-backed American Windsor chairs, and a child's tea set sitting on a tray constructed of a copper penny with a rim, another example of Mrs. Thorne's ingenuity.

The portrait over the secretary was originally part of Mrs. Thorne's large jewelry collection, and the bottle containing a miniature clipper ship was one of her proudest accomplishments.

Mrs. Thorne said, "Finding perfection in miniature ornaments and bibelots conforming to the decorative style of each period is expecting the impossible. In my extensive collection of tiny objects which I have accumulated during many years of travel, I sometimes find just what I need to put here and there in various rooms. However, many of the ornaments have been made especially for the places they occupy."

The Cape Cod Living Room offers one of the most beautiful views outside the front door looking at a trellis laced with pink roses and a little stoop bordered with hollyhocks, delphiniums, and forsythia. Gardeners appreciate the miniature rooms because many show authentic replicas of period gardens.

(*See A12: Cape Cod Living Room, 1750–1850 at the Art Institute.*)

CARTER'S GROVE

Interesting tales are associated with some Thorne rooms inspired by historic homes. Carter's Grove, a plantation house located north of the James River, six miles southeast of Williamsburg, was owned by Carter Burwell. The walnut paneled Virginia Drawing Room of 1775, referred to as the "Refusal Room" has a quirky story. Apparently, George Washington proposed to a young woman named Mary Cary who was visiting the owner's daughter. Mary Cary refused, but Washington later met the wealthy widow Custis in 1757 and reportedly made a better match. Later, Thomas Jefferson proposed to Rebecca Burwell, the owner's daughter, in this same room. She also refused!

The drawing room contains reproductions of English and American Chippendale designs. The bull's eye mirror over the mantel is in the Empire style of a later period, but Mrs. Thorne often mixed styles to create an elegant room.

In the right hand corner stands a frame with an embroidery piece partially completed, another example of domestic life taking place in the room, giving the impression that someone has exited but will return shortly to finish the project.

Carter's Grove plantation is open to the public and can be combined with a trip to Williamsburg.

(*See A25: Virginia Drawing Room, 1755 at the Art Institute.*)

THE TENNESSEE ENTRANCE HALL

This room was modeled after The Hermitage, President Andrew Jackson's home. The house was originally built in 1819, but in 1836 a fire destroyed most of it. It was re-built in the Greek Revival style while Jackson was serving the country as its seventh president. Jackson, nicknamed "Old Hickory" for being a tough general, enjoyed the plantation home of an aristocratic southern gentleman while showing his politically correct "democratic" nature.

The spiral staircase and hand-painted wallpaper make this one of the most dramatic and exquisite entry halls. The colorful wallpaper was designed by the Parisian, Joseph Dufour, and was copied from one owned by the Art Institute of Chicago, similar in style to the original in the Hermitage. Wallpapers appeared before the 1700s and usually featured scenes similar to those depicted on tapestries. High-quality hand-painted wallpaper was available from China in the latter part of the 17th century, but it was very expensive.

During the 18th century, England and France became the leaders in European wallpaper manufacturing. As early as 1712, during the reign of Queen Anne, a wallpaper tax was introduced and not abolished until 1836. Towards the end of the 18th century, France was engaged in a lively trade, selling panoramic wallpapers to Americans. Hanging the wallpaper in strips in the entrance hall was a difficult task, but Mrs. Thorne's experienced craftsmen were up to it. The Hermitage, located in Nashville, Tennessee is open to the public.

(*See A31: Tennessee Entrance Hall, 1835 at the Art Institute.*)

THE LOUISIANA BEDROOM

The important trading center of New Orleans was owned by the French and Spanish until the Louisiana Purchase of 1803, which included the city of New Orleans, and all or part of 15 states and two Canadian provinces.

The Louisiana Bedroom, circa 1800–1850, reflects aspects of a French Quarter house, a plantation outside the city, and a home in the Garden District. Most of the furniture is in the Empire style, illustrating the strong French influence. The chaise lounge, or méridienne (to rest in the middle of the day when the sun reached the meridian) with a high headrest was popular in the grand houses in France during the early 19th century.

The mahogany-framed mirrors above the side tables to the right of the room have additions of gilt and pictures that Mrs. Thorne thought in keeping with the French style. This is an excellent example of two rooms from an entire home. The view from the boudoir with elegant ballroom chairs and four-poster bed gives you a glimpse of the occupant's lifestyle.

(*See A32: Louisiana Bedroom, 1800–50 at the Art Institute.*)

THE MIDDLETOWN PARLOR

Mrs. Thorne reverted to her roots when she created the Middletown Parlor of 1875–90. The name Middletown came from a study based on a town in Indiana, Mrs. Thorne's birth state.

The room contains a revival of Gothic, Renaissance and Rococo furniture and decorative details, some taken from issues of *Antiques* magazine. The foyer contains a hall tree used to hang coats, hats, and scarves, still found in entryways today. In front of the doorway is the platform rocking chair introduced in the 1870s. It remained stationary, preventing wear on the carpeting.

Mrs. Thorne was good friends with Colonel McCormick, owner of the *Chicago Tribune*. They socialized in the same set, and Mrs. Thorne found herself seated next to him at a number of dinner parties. On one occasion he asked her why there was no copy of the *Chicago Tribune* in her miniature rooms. Mrs. Thorne said she would be happy to include a copy of the newspaper if he would provide one. He did and this room contains a copy of the *Tribune* in the paper rack to the right of the mantel. On the floor is another personal item given to Mrs. Thorne. The steam locomotive was presented to her by her friend, Colleen Moore, creator of the Fairy Castle in the Museum of Science and Industry. Originally the locomotive was gold, but Mrs. Thorne painted it black.

In the midst of this old-fashioned room filled with knickknacks belonging to a typical grandmother, a telephone hangs on the wall to the left of the platform rocker, a symbol of the busy world to come.

(*See A33: "Middletown" Parlor, 1875–90 at the Art Institute.*)

After the American Rooms were completed they were exhibited in the Allerton Wing of the Art Institute of Chicago from October 1940 until January 1941. Visitors flocked to the exhibit in anticipation of viewing the

Mrs. Thorne in the Art Institute of Chicago. (Courtesy of Anne Thorne Weaver)

final set of rooms, the culmination of 15 years of work. They provided an opportunity to travel and view historic homes without the dangers of war.

Many people felt the rooms offered a comprehensive record of mankind's accomplishments equal to history books, but more interesting!

> ***Miniatures by Mrs. Thorne Thrill Reception Guests***
>
> "The Antiquarian reception at the Art Institute for Mrs. James Ward Thorne was far and away the most distinguished of the season.
>
> "It was a happening full of electricity, where guests crowded in early to see the American Miniature Rooms and stayed late. The party was set in those remote east rooms of the institute which, while circling around formal courts and walled gardens, are reached via galleries galore, embracing treasures of the past. One had only to bat an eyelash to see en route the most perfect examples of tapestry, mirrors, porcelain and period furniture in existence.
>
> "Receiving at the far end was Mrs. Philip Miller, handsome young president of the Antiquarians and granddaughter of Mrs. George Pullman, early day head of the same society.

Beside her, looking a vision in white hat, white furs, white bouquet on a black frock, stood Mrs. Thorne, creator of the lovely American Rooms we were streaming in to see."

Chicago Sunday Tribune
December 15, 1940

Not long after the American Rooms were completed the United States entered World War II. Eugene Kupjack joined the Navy along with thousands of eligible young men. Kupjack worked in the office of Naval Research making orthopedic instruments, and did not return until after the war. Mrs. Thorne worked with the Red Cross helping with nurse's training and Mr. Thorne served as air raid warden for their apartment building.

The American Rooms followed the schedule of the older Thorne Rooms, traveling throughout the United States to leading museums, principally on the East Coast. Mrs. Ladusca Wilson, technical assistant, accompanied the rooms, packing and unpacking each fragile little piece when they left one museum and arrived at the next. Each piece was wrapped in white tissue paper with the exception of the most fragile pieces. They were wrapped in red paper. Unpacking and setting up took two-to-three weeks, and one room was unpacked at a time.

"I feel like a hostess waiting for her guests to arrive every morning when it is time for the exhibit to be opened at 10 a.m."

Mrs. Ladusca Wilson
Pittsburgh Sun Telegraph
October 18, 1942

"At first I was afraid of the tiny things. But I've become used to them now and don't feel so awkward with my hands. I have studied the types of people who lived in the originals so the rooms have a personality to me and they seem like real homes."

From an interview with Mrs. Ladusca Wilson
The Baltimore Sun
May 16, 1943

During the war years Mrs. Thorne continued her activities with the Woman's Exchange, but the display windows of their Michigan Avenue shop took on a new look. Along with interesting hand-made items sold in the shop were a number of air raid essentials: a bucket, tin hat, garbage pail, and a shovel. These were provided by Mr. Thorne, who had accepted the job of air raid warden for their apartment building at 1500 North Lake Shore Drive, where they had lived since the late 1930s.

Mrs. Thorne added a few necessary items for comfort in case the Exchange customers had to take cover: robe, comfortable slippers, knitting bag, and for reading matter, a book written by Dr. Edward S. Collins entitled *Don't Be Afraid!*

In 1941 Mrs. Thorne donated all three sets of miniature rooms to the Art Institute of Chicago to become a permanent exhibit used for educational purposes. This donation also included monies for installation of the rooms and upkeep.

Shortly after the gift was made, the Art Institute sold the first set of rooms to IBM (International Business Machines Corp.). During the 1930s, IBM had been busy compiling a substantial art collection, including contemporary art from 79 countries, art of the Americas, watercolors from the 48 United States, historic costumes of the Americas and the great Leonardo da Vinci models. In 1948, the *XVIII ARTNEWS ANNUAL* recognized IBM for its great American public collection "where Education is a Way of Life."

The Thorne Period Rooms in Miniature were exhibited in the IBM Gallery at 16 East 57th Street in New York City before they began a tour of the United States which lasted for almost 20 years.

> "My favorite of the three sets of rooms has always been the first series. It was especially beguiling for an antique toy collector because it contained many of the toys and treasures from her earliest collections. The furniture in the Victorian Parlour came from an old English dollhouse. The stove and many accessories in the Summer Kitchen were toys. Mrs. Thorne recognized their imperfections as architectural models but was sad when the Art Institute sold them to IBM. She had given all three sets with no constraints, so she could not object. I asked if money was needed for upkeep or installation; she said she had provided for that. I rejoiced when some of the first set were rescued by her son and installed in the Phoenix Art Museum."
>
> *Mrs. William Redd Mahoney of Oak Park, Illinois*
> *Founding member of the National Association of Miniaturist Enthusiasts*

This is a transcription of a letter written in longhand on Chicago Tribune letterhead.

CHICAGO TRIBUNE

December 12, 1941

Dear Narcissa-

I can't begin to tell you what a really great achievement you have done in your wonderful rooms. I spend a long time with them yesterday and I honestly think the group of rooms is not only the finest exhibit, from the point of interest and of workmanship, than anything in Chicago, or, in fact, the whole world, so far as my knowledge goes. I hope you can sense some of the enthusiasm I feel. I bought some extra books to send to friends in New York and London.

The completeness of each room is like the work of a jeweler. Everything down to the minutest detail has been done with a beauty and fidelity that is a perfect joy to behold. Each little glimpse from a window shows how beautifully you have carried the work to the garden, the distant backgrounds and the indirect lighting. Really, I think you have a right to the acclaim that is paid to the great painter and sculptor. And what a beautiful way to teach interior decorating and architectural detail! I'm glad "Life" saw the importance and charm of those beautiful gems of artistry.

Of course I had seen the rooms at the Fair and was prepared for something very fine but not such a marvelous collection as I saw today.

My most sincere congratulations!

With best good wishes,

JOHN T. McCUTCHEON

Letter to Narcissa Thorne from well-known Chicago Tribune *cartoonist John T. McCutcheon complimenting her on the great achievement of her Miniature Rooms. (Courtesy of Anne Thorne Weaver)*

When the Thorne Miniature Rooms were donated to the Art Institute in 1941, well-known cartoonist and friend, John McCutcheon of the *Chicago Tribune*, designed a drawing honoring Mrs. Thorne. It appeared on the front page on January 12, 1941 entitled "A New Art Joins the Old Masters at the Art Institute of Chicago."

Memorial to Mr. James Ward Thorne for his generous contribution to the School of Nursing at Passavant Hospital. (Courtesy of Susan Sacharski, Archivist at Northwestern Memorial Hospital)

CHAPTER 7

PHILANTHROPY

"We make a living by what we get.
We make a life by what we give."
Winston Churchill

Mrs. Thorne started her volunteer career at the age of 15 when she worked at a Christmas Bazaar for the Service Club of Chicago in December of 1897. By the time of her marriage in 1901, charity work had become part of her life. She was actively involved in the Art Institute of Chicago, the Chicago Historical Society, Passavant Hospital (now Northwestern Memorial Hospital) and Children's Memorial Hospital, but the Woman's Exchange continued to be the charity closest to her heart. The Woman's Exchange Movement, started in 1832, is one of the country's oldest continuously operating charitable organizations. Established in Chicago in 1893, it provided a means of livelihood or a supplemental income for many women who were unable to perform regular work outside of the home. The women sold a variety of hand-made items on consignment. The Exchange combined elements of entrepreneurship and charity.

Members of the Exchange hosted bazaars, receptions, and sales throughout the year, selling a wide variety of merchandise, some of which were donated by Exchange members. An article in the *Chicago Tribune* in January 1912 talked about "How to Earn Money at Home in Spare Time," encouraging women to participate in the Woman's Exchange. As early as 1916 Mrs. Thorne, as well as other members of the organization, hosted sales in their own homes to benefit the Exchange. By the 1920s and 1930s sales were often held at the Exchange shop at 902 North Michigan Avenue. Mrs. Thorne's exquisite Georgian dollhouse, created in 1932, graced the shop window and attracted large crowds of adults and children. Remarks such as, "See the tiny tea set?" and "Wouldn't it be fun to sleep in a bed like that?" were heard as the excitement of the

Passavant Christmas Bazaar selling shadow boxes designed by Mrs. Thorne, 1960.
(Courtesy of Susan Sacharski, Archivist at Northwestern Memorial Hospital)

upcoming Christmas Bazaar increased. Who would be the proud owner of the elaborate dollhouse?

For over 15 years Mrs. Thorne donated numerous dollhouses to the Exchange with rooms of varying styles: French bedroom, English library, French dining room and formal salon. On a more whimsical note, she donated an interior of the home of *The Three Bears*, with Goldilocks fast asleep in Baby Bear's bed.

Members of the Exchange acted as hostesses and saleswomen at the Bazaar, selling items including children's dresses, bonnets, coats, table runners, shadow boxes, dollhouses, dolls, cradles, window displays, lamps, sachets, pillows, negligees, etc.

In 1932, as a special favor to the Woman's Exchange and all the families whom it helped support, Mrs. Claus made an appearance at the Crystal Ballroom of the Blackstone Hotel on Michigan Avenue, the preferred venue for the famous Christmas Bazaar. Mrs. Claus handed lollipops to guests aged 10 and under. This was her first appearance in Chicago, and she was easily persuaded to tell stories about her home, husband, and the family business.

During the Bazaar lovely young girls sauntered through the crowd modeling hand-made tea gowns made of cerise velvet and rose satin. Occasionally the girls forgot to stay behind the screens while changing and had to be reminded that sometimes men attended the Christmas Bazaar!

The village of dollhouses was the most popular display at the sale. They were made by young draftsmen in the New York firm of Delano & Aldrich, and were exquisite replicas of houses that had been designed by the firm's architects. The commission offered employment and experience to young draftsmen. Mrs. Thorne furnished some of the dollhouses, but others were left empty, leaving the fun of furnishing to the buyer. Proceeds from the numerous Bazaars enabled the Exchange to donate money to feed needy families for several weeks. Mrs. Thorne served as president, and continued to volunteer and financially assist the Woman's Exchange throughout her life until the Chicago chapter closed in 1960.

In May of 1933, Mrs. Thorne organized an exhibit entitled "Things in Miniature" held at the Ackermann Galleries to benefit the Children's Memorial Hospital.

The miniature exhibits donated by Chicago women were designed to appeal to children. A farmyard scene, a fox hunt, and garden scene were created using Mrs. Thorne's collection of miniature bronzes. The Peter Rabbit house was a particular favorite.

One of the exhibits was a miniature living room that included a backgammon set with small pills used for the pieces. The designer went to the corner drug store and demanded to see all kinds of pills. She chose the smallest and colored them!

During the Christmas season Mrs. Thorne provided immeasurable joy to the children at Children's Memorial Hospital as well as to the patients and nurses at Passavant Hospital. Because of her love of and passion for the Christmas season, Mrs. Thorne was asked by the Little Traveler Shop in Geneva, Illinois to give a speech about her ideas on decorations and giving.

Here are some excerpts from her speech.

Christmas

"Unlike most women I know, I never look upon the usual preparations for Christmas as a hardship. I simply love it. I anticipate that back-breaking period with the keenest delight, and always work myself up to a high pitch of childish excitement which never ceases to bewilder my husband. He marvels at the hardy perennial quality of my enthusiasm.

"The day before Christmas usually finds me in a hopeless state of confusion, but I like it that way. One year I attained perfection from the point of view of the efficiency fiend. By

December 1st my gifts were bought, wrapped and covered with a sheet in the guest room closet. It was the dreariest and most depressing sight to me. I felt no pride whatever in my achievement. That proved to be my most extravagant Christmas. By December 15th I was desperate. There was no delicious litter anywhere in the apartment. This preparedness was getting on my nerves so I started all over again. I took several more poor families from the Visiting Nurse list. I found in the shops all sorts of fascinating things that were not shown before the holidays, and I added these little extras to the gifts I had already done up so painstakingly and prematurely for friends and family. That Christmas Eve found me in my usual frenzy of 'doing up' and I was simply bursting with Christmas cheer.

"About three weeks before Christmas I push all of the furniture of the guest room into one corner, put up bridge tables, and prepare for the fun of doing up my gifts. I make a real study of it. I look over my boxes, see what sizes and shapes I have, and buy at Denison's or Marshall Field's any extra ones I need. This done I go to the ten cent store! When I walk through those portals I am like an old war horse smelling powder. I simply love that place. It's so full of surprises! If you go early enough, you find interesting wrapping papers, ribbons, and such a variety of ornaments.

"It is extremely interesting to see how much personality can be put into the wrapping of a gift.

"All through the year I keep a box of appropriate papers for every occasion. I gather all sorts of lovely ribbons and cards for these occasions. It is such fun to send a package that is dressed up appropriately, but it takes thought and a great deal of time.

"It isn't necessary to give lavishly in order to make someone happy. I once had six scratch pads so charmingly done up that they were outstanding among my many elaborate gifts. A Christmas card with a friendly message can give great pleasure and often touches one deeply.

"At the twilight hour on Christmas Eve I join a group and walk through the wards of Children's Memorial Hospital pushing the elaborately decorated stretcher bearing a

Italian crèche in the reception hall of Passavant Hospital donated by Mrs. Thorne. (Courtesy of Susan Sacharski, Archivist at Northwestern Memorial Hospital)

beautiful crèche. As we pass from room to room, darkened for the occasion, the many candles illuminating the crèche throw fluttering lights upon the little figures in the beds. When the childish voices join in singing Christmas carols I struggle to keep back the tears and hurriedly busy myself in selecting luscious lollypops for each patient. This is a beautiful way to be taught the spirit of Christmas.

Plaque honoring James Ward Thorne for establishing the School of Nursing at Passavant Hospital in 1949. (Courtesy of Susan Sacharski, Archivist at Northwestern Memorial Hospital)

"A week before Christmas I place a really old Italian crèche in the reception hall of the Passavant Hospital. It stands in the center of a big table with rich old brocade backdrops. On either side of the crèche are gold urns filled with white lilies. Tall candles burn day and night. I am told that it is a source of great pleasure to the patients who are wheeled in to see it, to many visitors, and hospital staff.

"I am trying to transmit to you my deep love of this beautiful season of the year when we should all wake up to the real joy of giving."

Mrs. Thorne was a long time member of the Woman's Board of Passavant Hospital and active in numerous fund raisers. Both she and her husband were interested in promoting medical services. When James Ward Thorne died in 1948 his will provided a bequest of $25,000 to Passavant Hospital. In addition he set aside $50,000 to be given to a charity of Mrs. Thorne's choice.

Passavant Hospital had pioneered in the education of nurses, beginning in 1898, but had discontinued nursing education in the 1930s. By 1948 there was a shortage of nurses, so Mrs. Thorne donated $75,000 to re-establish the school of nursing. Her aid enabled Passavant Hospital to open the new school named the James Ward Thorne School of Nursing in 1949.

The Senior Class of the James Ward Thorne School of Nursing of 1952 paid tribute to Mrs. Thorne for her generous contributions of time and financial support for the class.

> "Our greatest debt is to our benefactress, Mrs. Thorne, because to quote an old phrase, 'Without her we would be nothing.' She, through her great generosity and sincere concern, answered the dire need for nurses in the present shortage. We also couldn't possibly forget all the thoughtful things she has done for us in the last three years, such as decorating the lounge at Christmas with prized ornaments, and giving us dinners on holidays when we couldn't go home. And all the parties, and formals, she will never know how much it was appreciated."
>
> *Miss Shirley Green, President, Senior Class*
> *James Ward Thorne School of Nursing*
> *June 12, 1952*

In honor of Mrs. Thorne, the student nurses' library was named the Narcissa Niblack Thorne Library. Mrs. Thorne remained a generous patroness until her death.

In 1944, Mrs. Bryan S. Reid began her term as Passavant Hospital Woman's Board president and plans for a gift shop were begun under the direction of Mrs. Thorne and her sister, Mrs. Alden Swift.

It opened in November of 1947, and Mrs. Thorne made regular donations of Shadow Boxes to be sold at the shop. The gift shop continues today as a source of income for Northwestern Memorial Hospital.

Mrs. Thorne admiring a nurse's uniform modeled by Carola Mandel at Passavant Hospital. (Courtesy of Susan Sacharski, Archivist at Northwestern Memorial Hospital)

From the mid-1940s until her death in 1966, Mrs. Thorne worked in her studio concentrating on miniaturized garden scenes, storybook settings, and caricatures in diorama or shadow-box form to be given as gifts or sold at the Woman's Exchange. Periodically the items were sold by art dealers who made donations to Mrs. Thorne's favorite charities, such as Children's Memorial Hospital and the Visiting Nurses Association at Passavant Hospital. These original whimsical creations, using treasures she had collected from all over the world, were labeled "Architectural Fantasies" by Mrs. Thorne.

Student Nurses' Library at Passavant Hospital named in honor of Mrs. Thorne. (Courtesy of Susan Sacharski, Archivist at Northwestern Memorial Hospital)

Antique toy collector and miniaturist, Mrs. William Redd Mahoney, had many memories of Mrs. Thorne throughout her life. The following is an excerpt from her paper, "Remembering Narcissa Thorne."

> "Mrs. Thorne was a genius with scissors and paper. She snipped intricate foliage and details from old engravings and aquatints and layered them to form delightful 3D scenes and landscapes. She could mold a standing *Godey* (popular magazine of the day) paper figure into a seated one to be set in a shallow vignette with cut background and furnishings. She often had these mounted on the lids of boxes and the sides of wastepaper baskets. They were a tremendous success. With none of the restrictions of the model miniature rooms, she could indulge her imagination, and each was an original, with her own designs of furniture and decoration.
>
> "She started the Christmas sales at the Art Institute of Chicago, and they gradually evolved into the present impressive Museum Shop. I still have some of the old Valentine lace paper and German scrap I bought at one of the first sales. Mrs. Thorne had discovered them in Bavaria.

"All her life she enjoyed making gifts for her friends. Many of the elegant small hats she wore came from Bes-Ben, the famous Michigan Avenue milliner. She made a miniature of his jewel box of a shop, and stocked it with replicas of hats he had designed for her. It was displayed in the shop along with a fantastic Easter egg she had copied from one of Queen Mary's jeweled eggs."

Many awards and honorary degrees were bestowed on Mrs. Thorne during the 1930s and 1940s. The American Institute of Decorators, The American Institute of Architects, and Northwestern University were just a few to recognize her expertise in the field of architecture, interior design and decoration.

After years of touring, the European and American Miniature Rooms were given a permanent home in 1954. They are in their own gallery at the Art Institute of Chicago, made possible by an exceedingly generous gift from Mrs. Thorne. She was relieved that they were finally settled in a secure setting, and she did not have to worry about transporting and setting up her beloved rooms. She was always concerned that the rooms be installed in the correct manner. James Ward Thorne wrote in a letter to IBM on March 11, 1943, "Mrs. Thorne is very anxious to have the installation of the numerous small items made with extreme care and judgment. Mrs. Thorne has found out from experience that this cannot always be safely delegated to others. Her precise touch often means the difference between having everything just right or all wrong."

Queen Elizabeth II visited Chicago in July of 1959 and was personally given a tour of the Thorne Room gallery by Mrs. James Ward Thorne. The Queen was very familiar with one room in particular, the English Drawing Room of the Early Georgian Period, similar to the room Mrs. Thorne had presented to Queen Mary in 1937 when she attended the coronation of King George VI.

Once again she gave a private tour of the Thorne Rooms to Queen Ingrid and King Frederick IX of Denmark when they visited Chicago in October of 1960.

In 1959, Mrs. Thorne was unanimously appointed an Honorary Curator of Decorative Arts at the annual meeting of the Board of Trustees of the Art Institute of Chicago.

She had been named Benefactor of the Art Institute in 1942, and since 1943 had been a member of the Committee on Decorative Arts.

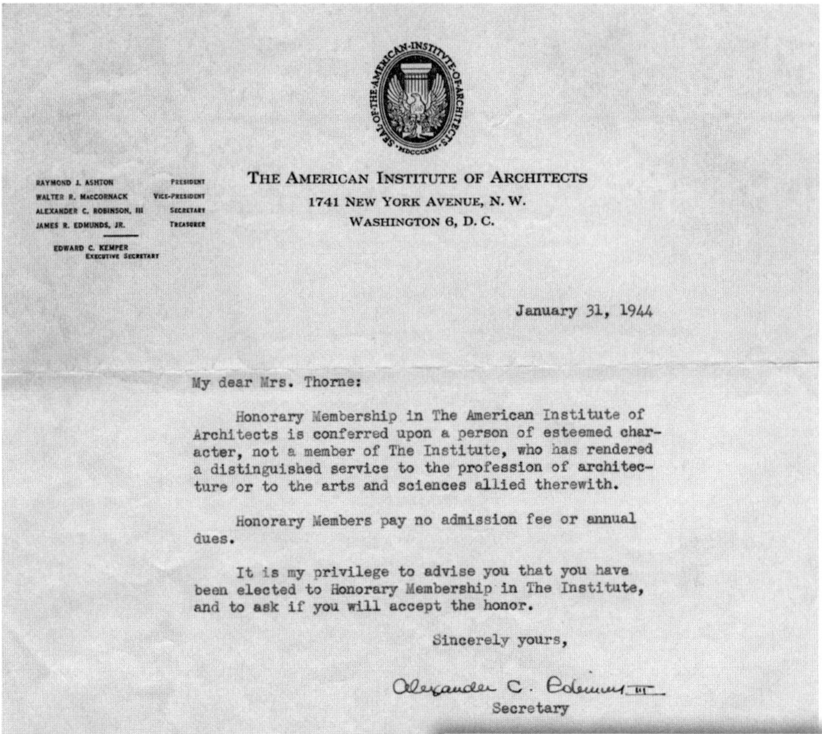

RAYMOND J. ASHTON — PRESIDENT
WALTER R. MACCORNACK — VICE-PRESIDENT
ALEXANDER C. ROBINSON, III — SECRETARY
JAMES R. EDMUNDS, JR. — TREASURER
EDWARD C. KEMPER — EXECUTIVE SECRETARY

THE AMERICAN INSTITUTE OF ARCHITECTS
1741 NEW YORK AVENUE, N. W.
WASHINGTON 6, D. C.

January 31, 1944

My dear Mrs. Thorne:

Honorary Membership in The American Institute of Architects is conferred upon a person of esteemed character, not a member of The Institute, who has rendered a distinguished service to the profession of architecture or to the arts and sciences allied therewith.

Honorary Members pay no admission fee or annual dues.

It is my privilege to advise you that you have been elected to Honorary Membership in The Institute, and to ask if you will accept the honor.

Sincerely yours,

Secretary

Mrs. James Ward Thorne
1500 Lake Shore Drive
Chicago, Illinois

ACR:ER

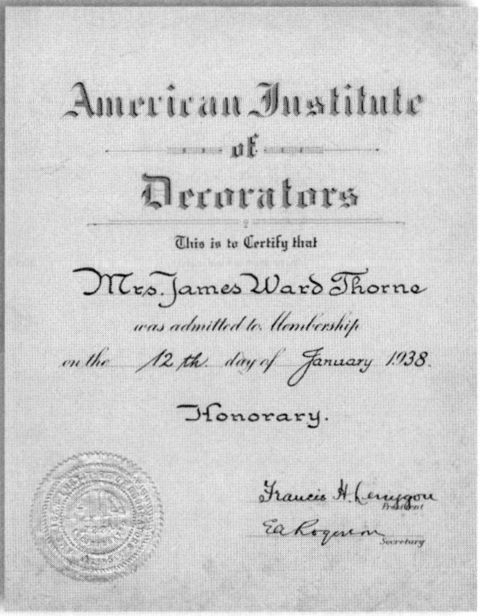

American Institute
of
Decorators

This is to Certify that

Mrs. James Ward Thorne

was admitted to Membership

on the 12th day of January 1938.

Honorary.

President

Secretary

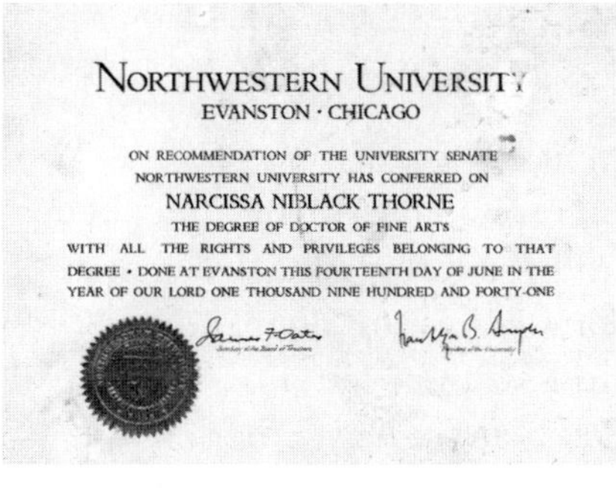

NORTHWESTERN UNIVERSITY
EVANSTON · CHICAGO

ON RECOMMENDATION OF THE UNIVERSITY SENATE
NORTHWESTERN UNIVERSITY HAS CONFERRED ON
NARCISSA NIBLACK THORNE
THE DEGREE OF DOCTOR OF FINE ARTS
WITH ALL THE RIGHTS AND PRIVILEGES BELONGING TO THAT DEGREE · DONE AT EVANSTON THIS FOURTEENTH DAY OF JUNE IN THE YEAR OF OUR LORD ONE THOUSAND NINE HUNDRED AND FORTY-ONE

Mrs. Thorne received many awards and honorary degrees including Honorary Membership in the American Institute of Architects in 1944. (Courtesy of Anne Thorne Weaver)

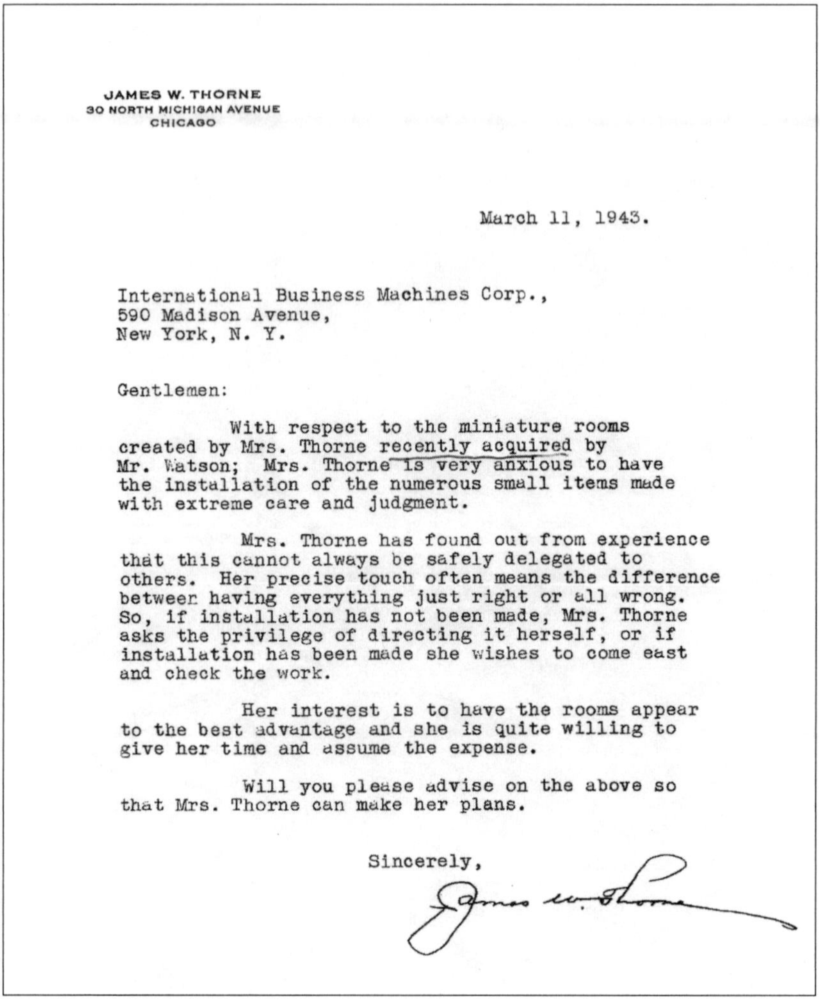

JAMES W. THORNE
30 NORTH MICHIGAN AVENUE
CHICAGO

March 11, 1943.

International Business Machines Corp.,
590 Madison Avenue,
New York, N. Y.

Gentlemen:

With respect to the miniature rooms created by Mrs. Thorne recently acquired by Mr. Watson; Mrs. Thorne is very anxious to have the installation of the numerous small items made with extreme care and judgment.

Mrs. Thorne has found out from experience that this cannot always be safely delegated to others. Her precise touch often means the difference between having everything just right or all wrong. So, if installation has not been made, Mrs. Thorne asks the privilege of directing it herself, or if installation has been made she wishes to come east and check the work.

Her interest is to have the rooms appear to the best advantage and she is quite willing to give her time and assume the expense.

Will you please advise on the above so that Mrs. Thorne can make her plans.

Sincerely,

James W. Thorne

Letter to IBM from Mr. James Ward Thorne in 1943 expressing concern about the correct installation of the Thorne Miniature Rooms. (*Courtesy of IBM archives*)

The new honor came as a result of her interest in the Art Institute, her benefactions, and providing a cultural history of furnishings, decoration, and architecture with her gift of the Thorne Miniature Rooms.

Curator of Decorative Arts, Hans Huth, wrote a letter to Board of Trustees President, William McCormick Blair, in November of 1959 documenting his admiration for Mrs. Thorne's contribution to the Art

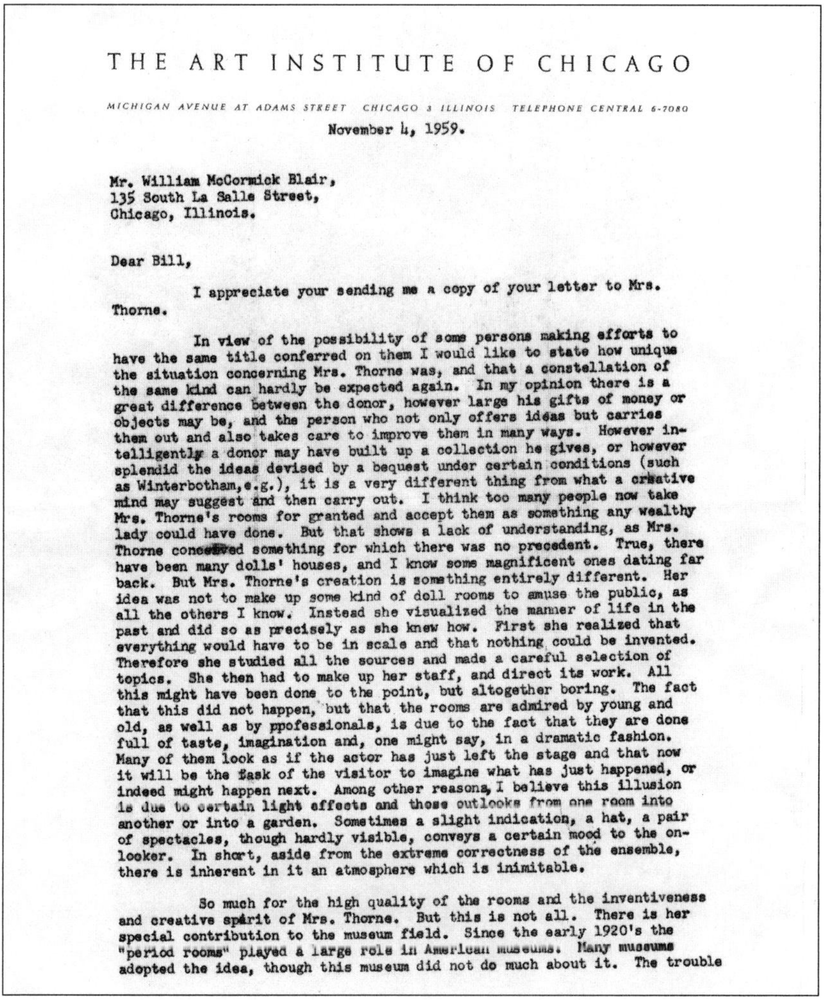

THE ART INSTITUTE OF CHICAGO

MICHIGAN AVENUE AT ADAMS STREET   CHICAGO 3 ILLINOIS   TELEPHONE CENTRAL 6-7080

November 4, 1959.

Mr. William McCormick Blair,
135 South La Salle Street,
Chicago, Illinois.

Dear Bill,

I appreciate your sending me a copy of your letter to Mrs. Thorne.

In view of the possibility of some persons making efforts to have the same title conferred on them I would like to state how unique the situation concerning Mrs. Thorne was, and that a constellation of the same kind can hardly be expected again. In my opinion there is a great difference between the donor, however large his gifts of money or objects may be, and the person who not only offers ideas but carries them out and also takes care to improve them in many ways. However intelligently a donor may have built up a collection he gives, or however splendid the ideas devised by a bequest under certain conditions (such as Winterbotham,e.g.), it is a very different thing from what a creative mind may suggest and then carry out. I think too many people now take Mrs. Thorne's rooms for granted and accept them as something any wealthy lady could have done. But that shows a lack of understanding, as Mrs. Thorne conceived something for which there was no precedent. True, there have been many dolls' houses, and I know some magnificent ones dating far back. But Mrs. Thorne's creation is something entirely different. Her idea was not to make up some kind of doll rooms to amuse the public, as all the others I know. Instead she visualized the manner of life in the past and did so as precisely as she knew how. First she realized that everything would have to be in scale and that nothing could be invented. Therefore she studied all the sources and made a careful selection of topics. She then had to make up her staff, and direct its work. All this might have been done to the point, but altogether boring. The fact that this did not happen, but that the rooms are admired by young and old, as well as by ppofessionals, is due to the fact that they are done full of taste, imagination and, one might say, in a dramatic fashion. Many of them look as if the actor has just left the stage and that now it will be the task of the visitor to imagine what has just happened, or indeed might happen next. Among other reasons, I believe this illusion is due to certain light effects and those outlooks from one room into another or into a garden. Sometimes a slight indication, a hat, a pair of spectacles, though hardly visible, conveys a certain mood to the onlooker. In short, aside from the extreme correctness of the ensemble, there is inherent in it an atmosphere which is inimitable.

So much for the high quality of the rooms and the inventiveness and creative spirit of Mrs. Thorne. But this is not all. There is her special contribution to the museum field. Since the early 1920's the "period rooms" played a large role in American museums. Many museums adopted the idea, though this museum did not do much about it. The trouble

1959 letter written by Hans Huth, Curator of Decorative Arts at the Art Institute of Chicago, to Art Institute Trustee President William McCormick Blair explaining how valuable the Thorne Rooms are to the Art Institute. (*Courtesy of Anne Thorne Weaver*)

Institute in the area of education by providing a history of mankind's domestic life for enjoyment by adults and children.

There is no way of calculating the total financial assistance she gave to numerous charities throughout her life, and inconceivable how much each Thorne Room cost to complete with approximately 134 items in each room. Her philanthropy was an exceedingly generous gift not only to Chicago, but to visitors from all over the world.

Mrs. Thorne at the Arizona Biltmore Hotel circa 1949–52. (Courtesy of Anne Thorne Weaver)

CHAPTER 8

THE STORY CONTINUES

"Narcissa, you lead a double life,
a big one and a little one."
Chicago Sun Times
March 20, 1966

Throughout her life, Mrs. Thorne was always happiest when immersed in a challenging project. In 1960 at age 78, her son, Bill, asked her to refurbish a number of Thorne Rooms originally sold to IBM by the Art Institute of Chicago in 1942.

The "tired rooms" had been traveling for almost 20 years and were in desperate need of attention. The task was a welcome challenge.

Mrs. Thorne contacted Eugene Kupjack who had been busy working on a commission for the American Institute of Decorators. Kupjack accepted the challenge and they tackled the restoration job with the same enthusiasm they had when creating the 37 American Rooms.

Completed in October of 1962, 16 rooms from the first set of 29 that the Art Institute of Chicago had sold to IBM in 1942, were ready to be installed in the Phoenix Art Museum in memory of Marie Thorne, Bill Thorne's deceased wife. Phoenix's fabulous "Fairyland" was opened to the public on November 1, 1962, and has been a popular exhibit since that time.

Fairyland to Open

"Today, at the Phoenix Art Museum, Bill Thorne is busily assembling the tiny rooms for the opening champagne reception on October 31. Working from photographs and diagrams, he is picking out tiny chess sets, minuscule books (hand-tooled and leather-bound), little statues and small tapestries, putting together the Jacobean Hall with its brass-weight little clock that actually keeps time, Louis XVI salon, the Directoire

Shadow box donated to the Woman's Athletic Club by Mrs. Gertrude Kemper. (Courtesy of the Woman's Athletic Club)

room, the Breton kitchen with its bowl of apples, and its wood box full and ready for the pheasant.

"Every detail in the rooms has been researched by Mrs. Thorne. The wallpapers have been copied, manufactured on an exact scale, the Gobelins tapestries woven from their parent tapestries, even the newspapers micro-copied and readable with a microscope.

"There is a real Ward's catalogue (who could resist that?); half-finished knitting in the knitting bowl of the Lodge Kitchen; even the carpeting and upholstery have been faithfully copied and woven to scale.

"When her world-wide searches failed, Mrs. Thorne invented. Tires from toy autos are donuts in a cookie jar; a Spanish comb is the carved back of a bed; a watch crystal becomes a mirror; and an old ermine collar is now a fur rug."

Maggie Savoy
The Arizona Republic
October 22, 1962

Dining room—example of a room designed for a personal friend.
(Courtesy of Suzanne Garvin)

Also in 1962, IBM gave nine of the first set of Thorne Rooms to Knoxville's Dulin Gallery, now the Knoxville Museum of Art. These rooms contain many of Mrs. Thorne's treasures from her earliest years of collecting. Restoration of the rooms was underwritten by Sherri Lee in honor of Mrs. McAfee Lee. They have been on display since 1965.

Mrs. Thorne continued to work in her studio creating shadow boxes, dioramas and gifts for friends until her death in 1966 at the age of 84. Always involved in the creative process, Mrs. Thorne's letter to her granddaughter, Anne, in 1965 mentions her frustration over not feeling well enough to travel, and how difficult it is to grow old!

In the early 1960s, Mrs. Thorne donated a series of miniature rooms to Presbyterian St. Luke's Hospital in Chicago for display in the children's ward. She gave 30 rooms to Russell Button Gallery (formerly Ackermann's) to be auctioned and monies donated to some of her favorite charities. In March of 1966 she closed her studio doors for the last time and donated the remaining items to Eugene Kupjack, her friend and co-worker. The contents included a German Hallway Thorne Room.

German Hallway designed by Mrs. Thorne on loan to the Art Institute by Hank and Jay Kupjack. (Courtesy of Hank Kupjack)

End of an Era of "Little Rooms"

"Thirty-five years ago a friend told Mrs. James Ward Thorne, 'Narcissa, you lead a double life, a little one and a big one.' It was a remarkably perceptive observation then and it has proved to be even more accurate with the passing years.

"Now, however circumstance has enforced a substantial change in Mrs. Thorne's double life, and we all are the poorer for it.

"Mrs. Thorne's little life was made up of literally hundreds of thousands of hours she spent creating her celebrated miniature rooms, a medium for which she has earned international recognition as an artist of incomparable talent. This unique endeavor has, for the time being at least, come to an end. Mrs. Thorne has disposed of her vast store of tiny treasures and closed the last of her studios. Characteristically, she has given everything to charitable causes.

"For many years Mrs. Thorne maintained her studio at the Woman's Exchange on North Michigan Avenue. One of the pillars of that shop, she also designed all the children's dresses, bonnets and coats, the dainty little pillows, the fine tea cloths, and table runners. And she did the shop's shadow boxes and created all the enchanting window displays.

"When the Exchange closed in 1960, Mrs. Thorne transferred her studio to an apartment in the 900 N. Michigan building where she continued to work 10 hours a day, often on Saturday and Sunday."

Jane Gregory
Chicago Sun Times
March 20, 1966

Mrs. Thorne died quietly at home at 232 East Walton Street in Chicago on June 25, 1966. Newspapers across the country paid tribute to a rare woman of artistic talent who provided so much joy to thousands of people through her philanthropic work and her creation of the miniature rooms. For Narcissa Thorne, the rooms provided a fascinating focus and purpose to her life. Through the years when so many women were finding their main solace in memories, she was still actively involved in artistic pursuits.

Services were held in the Westminster Chapel of the Fourth Presbyterian Church. She was buried at Rosehill Cemetery Mausoleum along with the Montgomery Ward and George Thorne families. The ornate patterned bronze gates for the Mausoleum were designed by Marie Zimmerman in 1926. Mrs. Thorne was so pleased with the artist's work that she commissioned Zimmerman to create the wrought iron work, lighting fixtures, and altar fitments displayed in the model Gothic English Church, "Our Lady Queen of Angels," part of the permanent Thorne collection at the Art Institute of Chicago. (*See E-29: English Roman Catholic Church in the Gothic Style, 1275–1300 at the Art Institute.*)

After her death the miniature rooms continued to be a popular attraction. Numerous technical assistants have taken care of the rooms over the years, but one particular personality stands out. Alice Pirie Hargrave Wirtz grew up in a family of collectors, and enjoyed antiquing around the world. Alice said, "I've always loved miniatures."

As a young married woman she met Mrs. Thorne through her mother-in-law, Colleen Moore Hargrave, creator of Colleen Moore's Fairy Castle at Chicago's Museum of Science and Industry. Wirtz's parents had given her several Mrs. Thorne rooms that they had purchased at the Woman's Exchange. It was exciting for her to meet the creator.

Wirtz started volunteering at the Art Institute for the Needlework and Textile Guild. During the late 1970s many rugs originally made for the American Rooms had to be replaced. The originals were made from antique cashmere and paisley shawls glued to a backing. After exposure to the heat of light bulbs for 35 years, the fabric started to separate. Research was carried out to create designs appropriate for each room. Alice, a needlepoint designer, was asked to design the rug for the anteroom of the Charleston Drawing Room as well as a tapestry for the Louis XIV Room. Guild members worked diligently to complete the rugs which took a total of 1,157 hours!

Alice Wirtz started spending more time in the Thorne Rooms and became the natural successor when technical assistant Anderegg resigned in 1978. She enthusiastically took over the job as custodian of the rooms, keeping a file on each room with original drawings and blueprints.

She arrived early to make the rooms ready "for the King and Queen to come," admitting she was a little more than particular. She donned a smock and took her supply cart through the gallery inspecting for

An example of the exceptional work being done today in the Miniature World designed by Sophia Twaddell, Miniaturist and author. (*Courtesy of Sophia Twaddell*)

smudges, fallen objects, and light bulbs that needed replacing. "It is as though little ghosts were in the rooms."

Caring for the Thorne Rooms "is a labor of love," said Wirtz in an article from the *Sunday Herald,* March 23, 1980, entitled "Housekeeping in Miniature: It's Work!" by Deborah Donovan. Spring cleaning was especially difficult. All items had to be removed from the rooms and the windows washed in vinegar.

Wirtz retired from her custodian job in 1991, but has remained enthusiastic and interested in the Thorne Rooms and their future.

During the late 1980s the Art Institute Board of Trustees offered members and friends of the Institute the special opportunity to dedicate a Thorne Room for $15,000 paid over a three year period. The commitment assisted in underwriting the construction, maintenance, and operational costs of the gallery. Plaques were placed under the rooms honoring donors who participated in the project.

In 1985, the Thorne Rooms were closed for four years for major renovation and conservation. The gallery was completely renovated by Skidmore, Owings, & Merrill and reopened in 1989.

In 2010, Conservation Technician and Research Assistant Lindsay Mican Morgan and her team of experts began decorating selected Thorne Rooms for the holidays. They researched traditions for the time periods of the rooms and found a miniature créche for the French Provincial Room, a Christmas tree for the English Victorian Room, a Hanukkah celebration for the 1940s California interior and a beautiful white ball gown for the Louisiana Bedroom, to name a few. Morgan and world-renowned artisans crafted many of the festive miniature decorations, which bring the spirit of the season to the Thorne Rooms. Ms. Morgan noted, "It was a time of year Mrs. Thorne cherished and I felt something should be done in her exquisite taste to honor and bring back a little of that grandeur." The annual exhibit has become one of the most popular at the Art Institute, and hopefully it will continue for many years to come.

The world of Miniatures is alive, well, and thriving throughout the world. Workshops attract large numbers of people pursuing a business in the miniature trade. To others it is a fascinating hobby. Every manner of class is offered from wiring a dollhouse to upholstering a chair.

Today you may visit the Art Institute to view the fascinating permanent collection of 68 Thorne Rooms which continue to bring a sense of wonder and amazement.

"It is certainly an exciting hobby," an interviewer once remarked. "Hobby?" laughed Mrs. Thorne, "it's a mania!"

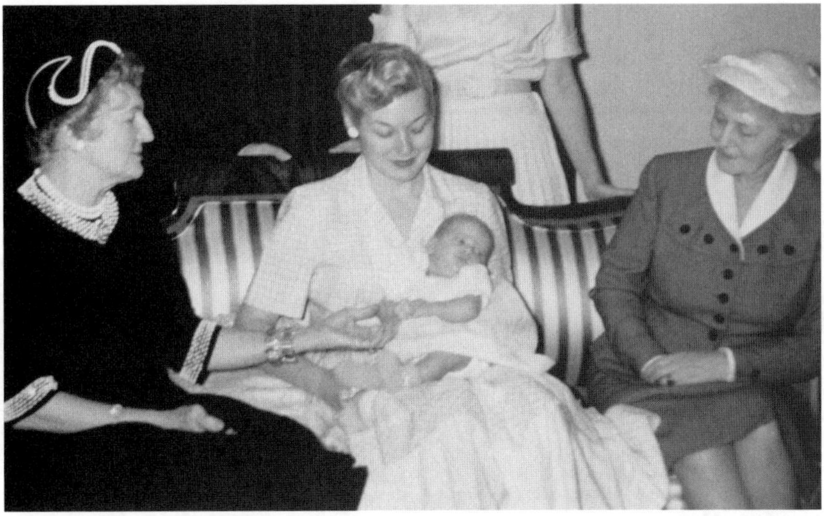

Narcissa Thorne (far left) looking at her granddaughter, Anne Thorne Weaver, holding her great granddaughter, Wendy. On the far right is the maternal great grandmother, Anna Hubbell. Des Moines, 1953. (Courtesy of Anne Thorne Weaver)

TIME LINE

1901

Narcissa Niblack married James Ward Thorne.

1910

Thornes commissioned Edwin Clark to design a country house in Lake Forest.

1926

James Ward Thorne retired from Montgomery Ward & Company. Travels to Europe increase.

1932

Rooms exhibited in New York to benefit the Architects Emergency Relief Fund.

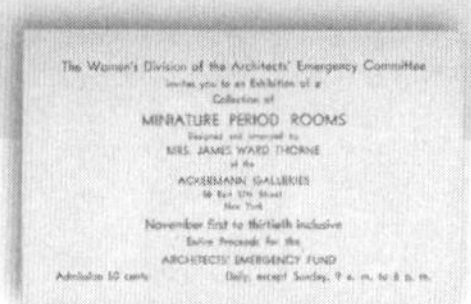

The Women's Division of the Architects' Emergency Committee
invites you to an Exhibition of a
Collection of
MINIATURE PERIOD ROOMS
Designed and arranged by
MRS. JAMES WARD THORNE
at the
ACKERMANN GALLERIES
[illegible]
New York
November first to thirtieth inclusive
Entire Proceeds for the
ARCHITECTS' EMERGENCY FUND
Admission 50 cents
Daily, except Sunday, 9 a. m. to [illegible] p. m.

1933

Twelve miniature rooms exhibited at the Century of Progress World's Fair.

1934

Twenty-six miniature rooms exhibited at the Century of Progress World's Fair.

1940

Thorne Miniature Rooms exhibited at the New York World's Fair.

1940-41

Third set of 37 American Rooms completed and exhibited in the Allerton Wing of the Art Institute.

1941

Mrs. Thorne donated all three sets of Miniature Rooms to the Art Institute of Chicago.

1949

James Ward Thorne School of Nursing established.

1954

Miniature Thorne Rooms given a permanent home in their own gallery at the Art Institute of Chicago.

1959

Mrs. Thorne became Honorary Curator of Decorative Arts of the Art Institute of Chicago.

1928

Edwin Clark commissioned to design a house in Santa Barbara.

1930

Mrs. Thorne purchased two chandeliers that became the inspiration for the first miniature room.

1932

Ten miniature rooms exhibited for the first time at the Ackermann Galleries in Chicago to benefit the Architects Emergency Relief Fund.

1937

Mrs. Thorne presented Queen Mary with a gift of a miniature Georgian library.

1937-8

Second set of 31 European Rooms completed and exhibited at the Historical Society of Chicago.

1939

Thorne Miniature Rooms exhibited at the Golden Gate Exposition in San Francisco.

1942

Art Institute of Chicago sold the first set of rooms to IBM.

1944

Mrs. Thorne given Honorary membership in The American Institute of Architects.

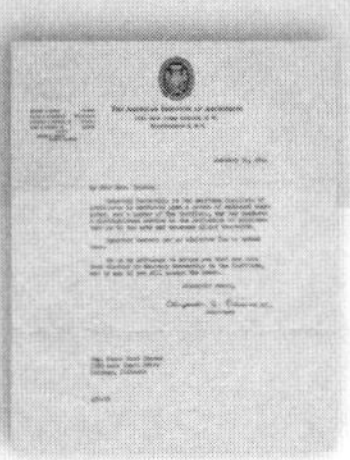

1948

James Ward Thorne dies.

1962

Sixteen of the first set of Miniature Rooms were refurbished by Mrs. Thorne and donated to the Phoenix Art Museum.

1966

Mrs. James Ward Thorne dies.

BIBLIOGRAPHY

BOOKS & ARTICLES

Boorstin, Daniel. "Montgomery Ward's Mail-Order Business." *Chicago History*, The Chicago Historical Society, Spring-Summer, 1973.

Brown, Vernon K. "The Story of Passavant Memorial Hospital 1865 to 1972." *Chicago*, Northwestern Memorial Hospital, 1976.

Buckland, Gail. *The White House in Miniature*. New York: W. W. Norton & Company, 1994.

Casey, Leo. (Director of Publicity) "News Release No. 701." New York: World's Fair of 1940.

Dollhouse Miniatures Magazine.

Fields, Mary Durland. "The Phoenix Thorne Rooms." *Miniature Collector*, February, 1982.

Finnegan, Stephanie. *The Doll House Book*. New York: Black Dog & Leventhal, 1999.

Fyler, Harriet Morgan. "An Exhibit Reminiscent of Fairyland." Chicago: The Art Institute of Chicago, 1938.

Harris, Neil. *Chicago Apartments: A Century of Lakefront Luxury*. New York: Acanthus Press, 2004.

Kelley, Charles Fabens. "Mrs. Thorne's New Miniature Rooms at the Art Institute." Chicago: The Art Institute of Chicago, 1938.

Miller, Donald L. *City of the Century*. New York: Touchstone, 1997.

Millhauser, Steven. "The Fascination of the Miniature." *Grand Street*. May, 1984.

Musgrave, Clifford. *Queen Mary's Dolls' House*. Andover: Pitkin Pictorials, 1978.

Rima Lunin Schultz and Adele Hast, eds., *Women Building Chicago 1790–1990*. Bloomington: Indiana University Press, 2001.

Rogers, Elaine. "How Mrs. Thorne's Rooms Came to Be." Chicago: The Art Institute of Chicago, 1937.

Rogers, Meyric R. *American Interior Design: The Traditions and Development of Domestic Design from Colonial Times to the Present*. New York: W. W. Norton & Company, 1947.

Rogers, Meyric R. "Gift of Sixty Miniature Rooms by Mrs. James Ward Thorne." *Bulletin*. Chicago: The Art Institute of Chicago (December 1941): 108–110.

Schrenk, Lisa D. *Building a Century of Progress: Architecture of Chicago's 1933–34 World's Fair*. Minneapolis: The University of Minnesota, 2007.

Stewart-Wilson, Mary. *Queen Mary's Dolls' House*. New York: Abbeville Press, 1988.

"The Carlisle Collection of Miniature Rooms: Nunnington Hall." Washington, D.C.: The National Trust, 1979.

The Miniature Collector Magazine.

Thorne, Mrs. James Ward. *Miniature Rooms: Official Catalog*. Boston: The Museum of Fine Art, 1940.

Thorne, Mrs. James Ward. *Miniature Rooms*. Phoenix: The Phoenix Art Museum, 1972.

Thorne, Mrs. James Ward. "Slides: Period Rooms in Miniature." International Business Machines Corporation, Collections of IBM's Department of Arts & Sciences, 1959.

Thorne, Suzanne. "Mrs. James Ward Thorne Miniature Rooms in the Permanent Collection of The Phoenix Art Museum." *Arizona Highways*, November, 1972.

"Thorne Room Miniatures." *Business Machines* (IBM Publication) Vol. 37, No. 2, 1954.

Tom D. Jones to L. H. La Motte. "Local Exhibits of Collections from the IBM Fine Arts Department" (Photocopy). IBM's Fine Arts Department, May 5, 1956.

Weingartner, Fannia. *Miniature Rooms: The Thorne Rooms at the Art Institute of Chicago*. Chicago: The Art Institute of Chicago, 2009.

UNPUBLISHED MATERIALS

The Art Institute of Chicago. *Thorne Rooms Scrapbook 1943–44*. (Ryerson Library, the Art Institute of Chicago) Number 15 (2001.138).

Thorne Weaver, Anne. "Scrapbook Relating to Thorne's Miniature Rooms."

Thorne Weaver, Anne. "Private Papers of Mrs. James Ward Thorne 1932–1940."

Thorne Weaver, Anne. "Testimonial Letters 1966–86."

INTERVIEWS

The author held interviews with the following people in the course of her research:

Carr, Peggy—Grande Dame of Chicago. (March 2013).

Freivogel, Caroline—Miniaturist. (July 2014).

Hilliard, Celia—Chicago Author and Historian. (July 2014).

Hindman, Leslie—Auctioneer. (August 2014).

Knepper, Rudy—Mrs. James Ward Thorne's Great-Nephew. (July 2014).

Krehbiel, Fred—former CEO, Molex, Inc. and Thorne Room Collector. (July 2014).

Miller, Arthur H.—Chicago Historian and Former Archivist, Lake Forest (Illinois) College. (June 2014).

Notz, John—Local History Buff. (December 2013).

Pollock, Colette—Miniaturist. (August 2014).

Tyre, William—Executive Director and Curator, Glessner House Museum. (June 2014).

Wirtz, Alice Pirie Hargrave—Technical Assistant, the Art Institute of Chicago Thorne Rooms. (July 2014).

OTHER RESOURCES

Leslie Hindman Auctioneers (Chicago) (www.lesliehindman.com)

Tom Bishop International Miniature Shows & Workshops (www.bishopshow.com)

Museums Housing Thorne Miniature Rooms

Art Institute of Chicago (111 South Michigan Avenue)

Phoenix Art Museum (1625 North Central Avenue)

Knoxville Museum of Art (1050 World's Fair Park Drive)

Indianapolis Museum of Art (4000 Michigan Road)

Museum of Miniature Houses (111 East Main Street, Carmel, Indiana)

Miniaturists and Restorers

E. J. Kupjack & Associates, Inc.
12 Main Street
Park Ridge, Illinois 60068

The Sixty-Eight Rooms Adventures

Written by Marianne Malone, Illustrated by Greg Call
Thorne Room Adventures for 8–12 year olds

The Sixty-Eight Rooms (Yearling)

Stealing Magic (Yearling)

The Pirate's Coin (Yearling)

The Secret of the Key (Random House)

Private Tours

Sally S. Kalmbach
sskalmbach@yahoo.com

ABOUT THE AUTHOR

SALLY SEXTON KALMBACH is a fourth generation Chicagoan whose family founded a coffee and tea company in the early 1880s at the same time Potter Palmer was developing Chicago's Gold Coast. Sally has taught classes in Chicago history at the Newberry Library, and has given numerous speeches and customized tours for individuals and small groups. Her expertise and ability to present material in an accessible, yet informative manner have resulted in a loyal following. Her topics include: Chicago's Gold Coast; Revisiting the Columbian Exposition of 1893; Mrs. Potter Palmer's Gold Coast; Women and the White City; Mansions and Millionaires: The McCormickville Walking Tour, offered by the Driehaus Museum; and Mrs. James Ward Thorne's Miniature Rooms.

Sally is a board member of the Chicago Chapter of the Society of Architectural Historians; a volunteer docent at the Charnley-Persky House Museum; and a fund-raiser for Opportunity International, which helps women in poverty start their own businesses.

Mrs. Thorne's World of Miniatures is the second in Sally's series on Great Chicago Women. Her first, *The Jewel of the Gold Coast: Mrs. Potter Palmer's Chicago*, has been a hit since its debut in 2009.

Private walking tours or speeches tailored to specific interests may be arranged. For further information, visit **www.chicagohistorytours.com** or email Sally at **sskalmbach@yahoo.com**.

"Going on a tour with Sally Kalmbach is an amazing adventure. Her depth of knowledge, and her joy in sharing it, make Chicago history come alive."
Kathryn Johnson